Bob Thomas

The Fail-Proof Enterprise

A Success Model for Entrepreneurs

BOOKS

© 2003 Bob Thomas

Published by IHC Books
33 East College Street, Hillsdale, Michigan 49242
800.437.2268

First printing 2003

Library of Congress Control Number 2003109722

ISBN 0-916308-50-2

Printed in the United States of America

Printed and bound by Edwards Brothers, Ann Arbor, Michigan

Editing, production & project management by **aatec publications**,
Ann Arbor, Michigan

Cover design by Hesseltine & DeMason, Ann Arbor, Michigan

To Ingrid, my wife and best friend

And special thanks to Sue Morrow
and Christina Bych, my editors

CONTENTS

FOREWORD

Bob Thomas writes that entrepreneurship is "a state of being."
He is himself in that state.

According to an old school of thought, nations tend to produce a certain type of character, a type related to whatever binds the nation together and makes it what it is. In a venerable literature, one may be adjured to "Act like a Roman," and it carries meaning.

Is it possible to "Act like an American?" Americans are famous for certain habits. They are thought to be pushy, loud, naive, welcoming. On a more serious level, they are known to be philanthropic and independent-minded, to have spirit for their community as well as an interest in themselves.

Americans also start businesses. They do it so frequently that it must have some cause written deep within them.

Giving an account of the way of "free labor," Abraham Lincoln once wrote: "There is no such thing as a freeman being fatally fixed for life, in the condition of a hired laborer...." Capital and labor, Lincoln goes on to say, cannot exist the one without the other. Labor is the superior of capital, because it is its source. He continues:

> The prudent, penniless beginner in the world, labors for wages a while, saves a surplus with which to buy tools or land for himself; then labors on his own account another while, and at length hires another new beginner to help him. This, say its advocates, is free labor— the just and generous and prosperous system, which opens the way for all—gives hope to all, and energy, and progress, and improvement of condition to all.

In a nation built to honor the principle of equality, it matters very much how ordinary people fare. Something in the American people gives them the energy, and what—in some nations—would be called the audacity, to strike out on their own, and ultimately to hire others to work for them.

The Fail-Proof Enterprise by Bob Thomas tells the story of how he did that. It gives advice to others who would follow in his footsteps. Just as in his business he provided great benefits for many people, so in this book he seeks to provide another benefit still.

In some ways this is a how-to manual. In others it is a reflection of the American character. As a businessman, a citizen, and a statesman, Bob is himself such a reflection. I expect you will enjoy this book, as I have enjoyed coming to know its author.

Larry P. Arnn
President
Hillsdale College

INTRODUCTION

Getting into business for one's self is easy. Remaining in business as a thriving enterprise is another matter, and therein lies the rub.

Most people have never had the chance to study the inner workings of a new business from start-up through the many phases that lead to a highly successful entrepreneurial enterprise. Small companies and their creators are rarely if ever profiled in leading business publications, such as *Fortune*, *Forbes*, or *Business Week*. Those magazines reserve their space to feature the leaders of our nation's largest and most influential corporations, the elite caretakers who never founded a business and built it from scratch with their own money. Even Lee Iacocca, who was perhaps the greatest automobile salesman of all time, and Jack Welch, ex-CEO of General Electric, were both born with aces back-to-back at Ford and GE. They had big budgets of company money to work with. But has either one ever started a business from scratch? No.

Without substantial funding, most Fortune 500 CEOs would not know where to begin, and I say that with no malice intended. The thousands of functioning entrepreneurial enterprises in this country are not only the seed for tomorrow's giants, collectively they represent a gross national product as great or greater than most of the big guys combined. We entrepreneurs are the backbone of the capitalist system.

This book was not written by an observer of other people's successes. I drew heavily on my own sales, marketing, and management experiences in order to show you the evolution of thinking that led to the creation of UNI-LOC, *the fail-proof enterprise.* I developed and utilized the organizational structure and management practices described here in the formation and operation of UNI-LOC and another very successful high-tech company, TBI (Thomas–Barben Instruments), both of which I founded with my indispensable partners. These were highly profitable entrepreneurial enterprises; now one is a division of a Fortune 500 company, Emerson Electric, and the other a division of the international Swiss conglomerate ABB. Because TBI was a clone of UNI-LOC, structurally and financially, this book will concentrate on UNI-LOC, which was perhaps the first enterprise of its kind to be owned, organized, and operated in this fail-proof way.

UNI-LOC, my first attempt at starting a business, began in 1964 as a liquid process control, electronic instrumentation company in Irvine, California. We were all young and had very little money, but we had a great idea. Our idea, however, was fraught with technical problems and an unidentified market—except for one blue-chip customer who would make all the difference *if* we could get our act together. Though inexperienced at running a business, what we newcomers did bring to the table was extensive sales and engineering experience, street smarts, and an obsession to solve some vexing technical problems to produce the most innovative instrumentation of its kind. And we did!

This is a "how-to"—and a "how not-to"—book for entrepreneurs. With an entertaining, case-study approach, it discusses funding, organization, sales, marketing, management, partnership compatibility, merchandising, control, lawsuits, patents, and selling out or going public at the proper time. And it shows you how my "Ten Essentials of the Fail-Proof Enterprise" actually work in the real world and why. It will guide you through the minefield of getting into business and, more important, successfully remaining in business *with very little money.*

What this book is not is some rah-rah motivational gimmick intended to fire you up to hunt lions with a fly swatter! Properly put to work in a new—or even an older—business, the fresh, creative ideas contained herein will prove priceless. This book is based on sound principles. It respects the basics of business, which, like the laws of physics, *cannot be abridged or dismissed* if maximum positive results are to be achieved. It will help minimize the luck factor when establishing and building a business, saving luck for those times when even the best prepared end up needing some.

I have assumed that prior to reading this book you have already decided what products or services your company will offer. I also anticipated that what you expect to find here is a method of organizing your enterprise to make it as fail-proof as possible with minimum financial risk. This book will do that.

First we show what it takes to be a genuine entrepreneur. Because sales is the single most important function of any business, we explore one of the highest levels of professional sales, and present a treatise on marketing. Then we investigate real marketing in its purest form, not to be confused with merchandising or computer "what if" games.

That is followed by advice on funding your new enterprise with very little money and without selling stock, without borrowing, and without accepting venture capital. Product development is thoroughly examined. This segment includes the story of some unexpected setbacks we encountered—inevitable in an entrepreneurial venture—that almost put us out of business shortly after we started, and what we did to overcome those roadblocks. Market identification and the methods used to penetrate that market once we defined it are detailed.

Then comes an in-depth analysis of the relative values of partnership skill contributions, which determines the number of company shares allocated to each partner.

Next I outline the most efficient *entrepreneurial* management structure, the one that will assure and protect your entrepreneur status for the longest possible time. We will look at the best way to assure partnership compatibility, while enhancing the success of your future middle managers before you give them management responsibilities.

Following that is an analysis of the strategies we employed to move our huge competitors aside and take over the undisputed leadership of our major market. Finally, we weigh the advantages of going public against those of being acquired. Should you elect to be acquired, we discuss how to protect the value of your newly acquired stock.

These are the highlights. There is much more.

While the fundamentals of organization outlined in this book apply to any business—beginning or established—they are primarily aimed at what I call the entrepreneurial envelope—enterprises with 20 to 200 employees. Why? Because depending on the kind of business we are talking about and the number of partners in active management, somewhere within that 20- to 200-employee envelope lurk the physical and mental limits that determine when the owners can no longer maintain personal control of their beloved enterprise. That is the time when they must succumb to that horror of horrors—the bureaucracy.

If an enterprise continues to grow, at some point it will surely become a bureaucracy or will be acquired by one—Thomas's First Law of Entrepreneurial Reality. This occurs when entrepreneurs can no longer properly perform all of the sensitive tasks themselves. Beside building a company that is monetarily successful, the next most important objective is to retain your entrepreneurial status for as long as possible in the interests of agility and efficiency-competitive advantage. This runs contrary to the views of many management consultants who call for building the bureaucratic management pyramid prematurely. But remaining an entrepreneurial enterprise without losing control requires special organization. An analysis of that organizational structure is a fundamental part of this book.

I was involved in one of the most exciting, perplexing, unpredictable, and rewarding business adventures any entrepreneur could hope for. And we had some fun along the way. I wish the same for you.

BOB THOMAS
Carson City, Nevada

CHAPTER ONE
ARE YOU AN ENTREPRENEUR?

What is an entrepreneur? The dictionary definition is "one who assumes the risk and management of business, enterpriser, undertaker." But there is much more to it than that. Entrepreneurship is a state of being. There are people who may think they are entrepreneurs and others who may act like entrepreneurs, but that doesn't mean they *are* entrepreneurs. During the past thirty years much has been said and written about entrepreneurship, and most of it comes up lacking. Unfortunately, but understandably, most colleges and universities know little about entrepreneurs, and consequently students are rarely exposed to that most valuable characteristic which is the cornerstone of private enterprise. These misfits, mavericks, malcontents, restless guns, troublemakers, whatever you want to call us—these entrepreneurs—are anathema to bureaucracy. And because institutions of higher learning are typically bureaucracies, as are all large corporations and governments for obvious reasons, their view is that the entrepreneur is someone to be put up with, not someone to be encouraged or taken seriously. It is typical of today's society to consider entrepreneurs greedy when in reality they are more often driven by the need to create and achieve.

The truth is, however, that almost every large corporation began as an entrepreneurial enterprise. Someone had an idea for a product or service and took a risk. By finding some way to finance the endeavor—by hook or by crook—sufficiently to demonstrate application and possible public acceptance, a little company was born. Henry Ford, my favorite entrepreneur of all time, is probably the most outstanding example of this. Old Henry controlled all policymaking and important management functions himself. Consensus decisions were not allowed. He detested middle management, which is the underpinning of bureaucracy. Ford probably holds the all-time record for having the largest number of employees while steadfastly holding onto his entrepreneurial enterprise. He personally juggled more balls simultaneously than any manager in history, much to the chagrin and frustration of his underlings who longed for the security blanket of the bureaucracy, and who were convinced that old Henry was crazy. Thomas's second law of business reality: "We usually despise those we need the most."

Doing Whatever Must Be Done

Not everyone can be an entrepreneur, no matter how hard he or she may try. If you are thinking about going into business for yourself, and you don't have a lot of money, you had better be sure that the prime mover in your new enterprise, the decision-maker, is a "take charge" doer. That person must be able to direct and perform as many different tasks as possible for as many hours per day as necessary for however long it takes. Such is the essence of the entrepreneur, being able and willing to do whatever must be done.

However, if you envision starting your new business as a bureaucracy, with enough middle management to assure that every function is adequately staffed by people whose areas of expertise and operation are clearly defined with little or no overlap, you will require an enormous reservoir of money. This is worlds apart from the typical entrepreneurial start-up where each participant wears several hats and does whatever needs doing. Bureaucratically structured start-ups are not common, except when a large corporation wants to initiate an autonomous division to explore some new market niche, such as the Saturn auto, or when stock underwriters issue shares in new enterprises with no track record, such as the recent proliferation of dot-coms.

Not all entrepreneurs are smart or even particularly gifted, no matter how enthusiastic or romantic their notions of independence and financial grandeur. The desire to be one's own boss is, of itself, not enough to guarantee success. When we work for a large company, it is easy to second-guess management and think we could do better because there is rarely much imaginative leadership in large bureaucracies. Big companies manage by consensus. And since employees rarely have a personal financial stake in the company other than their jobs, it is easy to criticize. But while large bureaucratic enterprises may be slow and unresponsive, that is what protects them against making brash, hasty, costly mistakes.

Consensus, or committee, management, is rarely notewor-
thy or brilliant, but it is relatively safe. As an entrepreneur, I
thank God every day for those plodding bureaucracies with
whom I have competed. They are the main reason there will
always be room for new small companies in the United States
(assuming that the government doesn't get more intrusive).
Entrepreneurs squeeze between the boulders, respond much
more quickly to customer needs and wishes, and reap the rewards, not the least of which are whipping the big guys in the
marketplace. There is nothing more satisfying than that, not even
a sweet-spot 300-yard drive.

How did I discover I was an entrepreneur? Quite by accident, and fairly late. I knew something was wrong during my
six years as an aircraft and missile systems engineer following
my graduation from UCLA, but for the life of me, I couldn't put
my finger on what it was. I was a good, savvy engineer for my
experience level, but somehow I didn't fit the mold. I was too
impatient. Government and corporate methods of assigning
tasks drove me up the wall.

My first job was with North American Aviation, Auto-
netics Division, where I worked for a physicist. We were immersed in the design of an inertial guidance system for an inter-
continental subsonic missile, the Navajo. The technical aspect of
the work was leading-edge but I felt underutilized, although my
lack of experience didn't dictate that I be given more responsibility. Engineering management, in my mind, wasn't remotely a
consideration or possibility.

My second job was in the same capacity for Northrop Aircraft Company, as fine a bureaucracy as one could ever want to

work for, on a similar project, the SNARK pilotless bomber. Again, I was technically challenged and I worked with some outstanding engineers, but I was unfulfilled. Something was eating away at me, making me increasingly difficult to work with. I had a reputation for being a good but impatient engineer. I felt driven with no place to go. This is a characteristic of the latent entrepreneur, but I had no way of knowing that at the time.

Suffice it to say I was lucky to come across the only bona fide aptitude testing organization in the United States, the Human Engineering Laboratory (more on this in the Epilogue). A three-day battery of tests showed that somehow I had to find a way to switch my career into, of all things, management, teaching, or sales. Well, there is no shortcut into management unless your wife is the boss's daughter, and even though I had taken the required courses at UCLA for teaching credentials, practice teaching at University Junior High School in Beverly Hills had killed any desire I may have had to do that. And I had never seriously considered selling, although I had made one exploratory attempt to get a sales engineering trainee's job a year or so earlier with Minneapolis Honeywell's Los Angeles office, which I didn't get.

I refused to tell the Lab what I did for a living until after I had completed the tests. During the debriefing, my counselor, Joseph Wallace, proceeded to describe all the frustrations I would experience if I pursued a career in engineering. He hit the nail on the head. He had just told me the story of my life. Then he suggested combining my high engineering aptitude with my sales personality aptitude into a career in technical product sales, selling high-tech products and/or engineering services to an industry I already knew—for example, aircraft and aerospace companies. After considerable thought, all of about ten seconds, I decided to re-explore that possibility. Wallace showed me that in sales engineering I could incorporate five of my strongest aptitudes into my work. The object of the aptitude game is to use your strongest aptitudes in your work and your next strongest in your hobbies or play. You no longer waste time with your low aptitudes.

Getting into Sales

I found that breaking into sales at the professional level was not easy. It wasn't like selling vacuum cleaners or automobiles. Sales engineers had called on me from time to time at Northrop, and I had a good feel for what was required. I also felt I would have a big advantage because of my engineering background because most sales engineers, while excellent salesmen, have limited technical experience. But be that as it may, the sales trait has to be predominant.

Luckily, the Lab put me in touch with a certain C. B. Buchanan, author of *How To Get a Sales Position*. He was a sales consultant who specialized in turning inexperienced people like me into salesmen; he taught me how to get a professional sales job without previous experience. I worked with Buchanan one night a week for three months. At the end of that time, under his tutelage, I wrote letters to the presidents of five local companies that engineered and manufactured aerospace products that were up to my standards. I got five interviews and received five job offers. I wasn't asked one single question that I had not anticipated. On the downside, I did have to take a salary cut for six months, which wasn't easy with a wife and four kids. Sales engineers were not on commission, although I wish I had been. We were on salary plus expenses, a car allowance, and possible bonuses. I took to sales engineering like flies to horses.

Sales is of an entrepreneurial nature, and it is probably the best training ground for general management. Different kinds of sales situations can positively or negatively affect your business—depending on your actions. If you are an engineer, an accountant, an MBA, or a factory superintendent you will undoubtedly think otherwise. But like it or not, sales is the most important single function of any business enterprise.

To paraphrase the late great Red Motley, known in the 1950s as the world's greatest salesman: "Nothing happens until somebody sells something." Ponder that statement for a moment and see if you can picture what he means. And no, the Internet has not diluted "Motley's Law" one little bit. If anything, it has brought it into sharper focus. For example, you may think automobiles are manufactured before they are sold, but they are not. Dealers order and contract to buy those cars before they are built. The cars have been pre-sold to the dealers. This means that the dealers have had to determine what models they think they can sell to you and me. They are the last guys on the chain, and they had better be right.

The Internet companies, which for the most part warehouse merchandise, often contract to buy that merchandise well before most of it has been manufactured. Manufacturing companies don't stock their own goods very far in advance of sales. Nobody wants to be stuck with unsold inventory. Again, nothing really happens until somebody in the chain sells something.

I want to stress that sales is without a doubt the only job within a bureaucratic company where a person is allowed and encouraged to function as an entrepreneur. If you have the aptitudes for sales, selling is the best means you will ever find to identify and develop your entrepreneurial skills and traits while working for someone else. Only in outside sales can you operate as a decisionmaking, quasi-entrepreneur within a bureaucratic environment, the only restriction being that you remain within the bounds of company policies. Why is it possible to operate so independently in sales? Because salespeople are the real risk takers within the bureaucracy. They have no place to hide. There is no way to cover up for lost sales or poor performance. And no intelligent sales manager is going to interfere much with his or her salespeople's operating methods for two reasons: (1) He wants to give his people room to grow, and (2) he doesn't want the blame put back on him if things go wrong. Micromanaging front-line sales personnel is the kiss of death to their ingenuity, creativity, and motivation.

In my case, there was no questioning my entrepreneurial characteristics and abilities after only a brief time in sales. I planned as an individual, made my sales calls as an individual, made my own strategy decisions, took my own risks, set my own hours, entertained whenever I felt it advantageous to the company, and controlled my own reports. The only thing hanging over my head was my sales quota, which was established by my boss. And that was fair enough. What better way to judge sales performance other than by achieving a quota, provided company policies and management objectives are met?

Again, I was fortunate. My employer was bureaucratic, but not stifling, and I had a great boss who was a fine teacher. Every year I made or exceeded my quota, doubling and tripling it. Eventually I was made Los Angeles regional manager. My earnings increased accordingly, but had I been on commission—"Mamma Mia!" Incidentally, two of my customers were North American Aviation and Northrop Aircraft Company, my old employers. What goes around comes around. My new relationship with the North American and Northrop people with whom I had worked took on a different aura. I was treated like a pro.

Interestingly, during that period I did not give one thought to being in business for myself. Why? I have pondered that over the years and concluded that I was happy as a clam in aerospace sales because I was already exempt from the constraints of company red tape. I was as close to being in business for myself as I could possibly be without actually taking the plunge. I could have easily slipped into the manufacturers' representative business, picking up eight or ten good product lines to sell, hiring and training some fresh young sales talent, and going out on my own. But I never seriously considered such a move, although I did file away in my mind the names of some great engineers with whom I would like to be affiliated should an unusual business opportunity come along. When I finally bit the bullet and founded UNI-LOC, it was more accidental than on purpose—my back was to the wall.

Essence of the Entrepreneur

If you are wondering whether you are the entrepreneurial type, a risk taker who thrives on solo performance, the best way to find out is to get into sales. It is vitally important that you know before you start your own business whether you have the aptitude to be the dominant entrepreneur. But that said, you are not required to have sales aptitudes or any stereotyped behavioral patterns to qualify as an entrepreneur. Scientific types, accountants, teachers, lawyers, doctors, and many others can be, and are, genuine entrepreneurs. But somewhere within your new organization there had better be someone who knows how to sell.

The characteristics of the born entrepreneur are drive and desire, enthusiasm, high-energy level, vision, some creativity, impatience with mundane details, disdain for red tape and unnecessary meetings and memos, and zero tolerance for wrong or dishonest answers. This does not mean that every partner in a new enterprise needs these characteristics, but the prime mover, the leader, must have them. Supporting partners can be comparatively passive. I mention this because, as you will see, I am bullish on partnerships; I have been a member of some beauties. I much prefer owning a lesser percentage of a thriving enterprise than 100 percent of a bomb.

CHAPTER TWO

SELLING TO PROFESSIONALS

The organization and management structure I devised for UNI-LOC grew out of my sales engineering experiences. During those years, and because of those experiences, I solidified my ideas on how, and how not, to organize our own business enterprise. Being in sales provided me with a platform to observe almost every aspect of our company's and our customers' operations.

I had the good fortune of working in sales for an outstanding high-tech company, The John Oster Mfg. Co., Avionics Division, and then in marketing for Non-Linear Systems, Inc., perhaps the most innovatively managed high-tech company of its time. Oster Avionics was a division of the famous appliance, barber clipper, and animal clipper company. Non-Linear Systems, or NLS, was the originator of automated analog-to-digital instrumentation, and the forerunner of Kaypro, a pioneer in personal computers. One was a rather informal bureaucracy, while the other was strictly entrepreneurial. Both were family-owned.

My days with the Oster Company were the happiest of my working life. My boss, Ward Carlson, was a great teacher and a born manager. He gave me the latitude I needed to develop my full potential as a sales engineer. There is no doubt whatsoever that both Ward and I would have cast our lifetime lot with Oster had not an unfortunate thing occurred, that is, from our point of view. John Oster, Sr., the founder and principal owner of the company, was getting up in years and was in ill health. John, Jr. had been running the appliance division for years—Osterizers, mixers, power tools, barber and animal clippers—and the other son, Bob, was managing the Avionics Division. Because of confiscatory death taxes that could have broken up the company upon John, Sr.'s death, John, Jr. and Bob were faced with either selling or merging the company for stock in a bigger company in a stock-for-assets transaction or going public with an Oster stock offering.

Of course, most employees were hoping against hope that the brothers would take the company public. Ward and I would have mortgaged everything we had to buy Oster stock, and I am sure most of the other employees would have done the same. But, for personal reasons, Bob and John, Jr. decided to do otherwise. Perhaps they were afraid John, Sr. might die before all the SEC red tape could be satisfied and a public offering made. Whatever it was, it must have been a painful decision. (Never did I dream that *I would be in the same dilemma myself within ten short years.*) The Oster Company was sold to Sunbeam of Chicago, an even bigger appliance maker. On paper the Oster–Sunbeam marriage looked ideal because together they could dominate the small appliance market. And they did. But something negative happened, and it seemed to those of us who were fairly close to management that neither Bob nor John, Jr. seemed overjoyed when dealing with the Sunbeam board of directors some months later.

I was in hog heaven with Oster before the Sunbeam acquisition. Even though the Avionics Division was fundamentally bureaucratic, the chain of command was short, especially in sales. My boss, Ward Carlson, reported directly to Bob Oster. I answered to Carlson, and the western sales engineers answered to me. Because of the more complex "systems" nature of the aerospace business generated in my region, I visited our engineering department and plant in Racine, Wisconsin, three or four times a year. There I had the opportunity to learn a lot from Bob Oster. The Avionics Division was a very contented family.

There was little doubt in my mind that someday, had the company gone public, eventually I would have become overall company sales manager and Ward the general manager. I could see Bob Oster evolving into more traditional presidential duties as demanded by a growing company. With that growth would have come more and more bureaucracy, like it or not. That is the inevitable price paid for success, and the Avionics Division was already inching toward that point of no return. Bob Oster did everything he could to keep the company functioning as informally as possible for its size. Long after I had left, and after severing his own ties with Oster–Sunbeam, Bob organized a new company. I noted with more than passing interest that he guarded his new entrepreneurship judiciously.

The Big Picture

What did I learn from the Oster experience? I got a Ph.D. in sales for one thing, but that wasn't the half of it. I learned how an organization functions day to day: The ongoing hassles, for example, with the engineering department over specifications and delivery dates for proposals, not to mention prototypes and final production drawings. Add to that the usual delayed delivery dates for production units when my customers were beating me over the head for parts. More often than not, my customers' customer was Uncle Sam, who has all sorts of penalty clauses in his contracts for delayed deliveries. Sometimes those penalties would be passed through to us. I learned about renegotiation. But all that went with the territory. In high-tech, especially aerospace, we game players were continually pushing the state-of-the-art: Time estimates and deliveries were educated guesses at best. But if push came to shove, those of us at the end of the chain were always at risk. There was never a dull moment.

While sales engineering incorporates the main elements of sales, it is really relationship selling. Technical sales never involves emotions because my customers didn't have "now attacks," the overwhelming passion to buy something on the spur of the moment. We were a technical support service out of which products were born to solve specialty engineering problems. Aerospace prime contractors like North American, Northrop, Convair, Douglas, Boeing, and Lockheed don't manufacture the systems or internal components that go into their aircraft or missiles. Those items are supplied by hundreds of subcontractors like

General Electric, Hughes, TRW, Honeywell, and Oster. Customer relationships are based on the subcontractor's—our—ability to solve their specialized problems. In my case, the typical gestation period that would result in a contract was twelve to eighteen months. Sometimes even longer, although Oster did have an off-the-shelf line of rotating components—synchros, servo motors, resolvers, and so on—that could be purchased on short notice. Understandably, these were management's favorites.

After working diligently with my customer's engineering departments for many months and helping to create and write the product specifications, and biasing those specifications in our favor as much as possible, the project would come out for open bid. Usually we would find ourselves bidding against seven or eight qualified competitors, most of them bigger than we were. Among my worthiest competitors were Honeywell, Fairchild, Kearfott, American Electronics, and Kollsman. Low bidder would almost always get the contract, provided the fine print conditions were met. About the only things that could disqualify the low bidder were previous nonperformance problems or financial instability.

Blind-Sided

Tragically, this "nonperformance" business surfaced with none other than my first employer, North American Aviation (NAA), with whom the Oster Company had a serious contract dispute three years prior to my being hired. I found out the hard way that we were in trouble when I went to the NAA purchasing department to pick up a copy of the just released B-70 (Mach 3 bomber) bid specifications, which I had worked on for more than eighteen months with NAA's engineering department. I was politely informed that Oster was on the "No Bid" or blackball list because of "failure to perform" on a F-86 fighter plane rudder trim actuator contract a few years previously, during the Korean War. I was stunned, embarrassed, angry, and determined to get to the bottom of this poorly timed catastrophe. I met with the North American engineering group that had the original project responsibility for the F-86 fighter to find out what they knew about the dispute. They had no knowledge of our being blackballed by purchasing and were very helpful, briefing me on the background from their point of view. Then I flew to Racine and examined Oster's records and documents, and finally put the pieces together. This was accomplished in three days.

What had happened was that North American's prime subcontractor, who shall remain nameless, had the entire F-86 actuator contract and had fallen hopelessly behind in its delivery schedule. Oster was called in as a last minute *sub*-subcontractor to help out, building actuators to the production drawings supplied by the *prime* subcontractor. This was the worst possible position to be in. Either the prime subcontractor or North American had made some production drawing changes along the way, and neither had sent Oster copies of the revised drawings. Consequently, the Oster-supplied actuators failed to meet the changed specifications and were rejected by the Air Force. F-86 fighter plane deliveries went to hell and Oster got the blame.

Because the Air Force was screaming for F-86s for Korea— without rudder trim tab actuators a large number of these aircraft were not flyable—the stops were pulled out to get those actuators rebuilt. Not only did Oster work around the clock for days once it was given the correct production drawings, it ended up in essence wrapping a $200 bill in losses around each actuator shipped. Many companies would have legally refused to continue under such circumstances without a new contract and price adjustment. Oster, however, hung in there. But neither North American nor the prime subcontractor, *who was the real culprit*, would admit responsibility and cover Oster's losses.

What is the best way to handle such a terrible situation? Do you make a claim and force the issue, embarrassing the customer and causing heads to roll? Or do you shut up and take it in the shorts? With the Air Force involved, which could sanction penalties against anybody and everybody, it was decided to let sleeping dogs lie. During the heat of the battle, thinking it may need a scapegoat, NAA purchasing blackballed Oster, branding the firm unacceptable as a future supplier. And someone at North American had failed to remove that impediment after the incident had been satisfactorily resolved.

Somehow I had to get the facts to North American's *purchasing* department at the highest possible level. I called the director of material several times for an appointment, but when he found out who I represented he was always too busy. So, I decided to camp on his doorstep. What did we have to lose that we hadn't already lost? A $6 million contract was at stake (in 1959 dollars). That was a worthwhile piece of business, definitely worth going the extra mile for—especially considering that I had worked on the project for the better part of two years already, and had helped write the specifications around Oster's strongest capabilities. This was our job!

When the purchasing director arrived for work in the morning I was there in his lobby. When he went to lunch I was there. When he came back from lunch I was there. And when he went home I was still there. We greeted each other every time, and it soon became somewhat amusing, at least to him. After two days of this routine he finally let me into his office and gave me the chance to outline with my documentation the entire actuator affair, which he scrupulously examined. Off the record, his own engineering department backed me up, confirming the production drawing changes. A couple of hours and a few in-house phone calls later, our meeting concluded with the understanding that the Oster Company had performed admirably under the circumstances, having spent more of its own money on the project than the original sub-subcontract was worth.

We were re-established on the active bid list as an approved subcontractor, and three months later, subsequent to the bidding and proposal evaluation processes, we got the coveted development contract for the jet engine monitoring system and instruments on the B-70 supersonic bomber. How sweet it was, although short-lived. It wasn't long after that the mass production part of the contract was canceled by Congress, even though a flying prototype had been built and tested. Its flight tests were phenomenal. Two thousand miles per hour in 1960. Probably one of the greatest aircraft of all time—destined for the political junkyard.

Nonetheless, there was a double sweetness to winning that contract. My main competitor, Honeywell, came in second in the evaluations. Just three years earlier, Honeywell had turned me down for employment as a sales engineer trainee because I had failed to pass its in-house psychological profile tests. I didn't conform to Honeywell's norm, whatever that was supposed to mean. The same Honeywell manager who had turned me down was present at the North American debriefing conference where, in front of him and his two sales engineers who had been calling on North American, I was awarded the contract in Oster's name. His reaction of surprise was duly noted. It was a nice day.

The Honeywell sales engineers who competed with me on the B-70 obviously had the "right" psychological stuff to suit Honeywell—but they lost the contract. They were surprisingly naive; when they made a sales call at North American I knew who they had seen, when, what was discussed, and how many times they went to the men's room.

There was a huge difference between the off-the-shelf psychological profile tests used by Honeywell and other companies in the 1950s and 1960s and the Human Engineering Laboratory's *aptitude* tests. Psychological profiles were a fad. There is no question that many good people were rejected for employment because of them. The test results were never given to those who failed to pass. And the tests themselves were very intrusive. I almost gave up on sales forever because of those Honeywell tests. I was fortunate in that I later had the opportunity to take the Human Engineering Lab tests and found, before it was too late, that I did indeed have ideal sales engineering aptitudes. But what of those many others, some of whom I knew, who weren't so fortunate? I am sure those so-called psychological tests did a lot of damage to a lot of people.

The B-70 was the most exciting project I have ever been privileged to be a part of. The official name for the big bird was the "Valkyrie," but the NAA engineers called it "The Savior."

Of course it was classified "secret," and even though I had a "secret" military clearance with roving badge privileges that allowed me to go most anywhere within the facility without escort, I still hadn't been cleared to view the full-size mock-up of the B-70. When I finally did get clearance, and the project engineer, Ben Peterson, took me into a gigantic hangar for my first glimpse, the first words out of my mouth were "Jesus Christ." Peterson laughed and said, "Now you know why we call it 'The Savior.'"

Lessons Learned

There is a great lesson to be learned here for any company, new or old. Never take anything for granted. I had neglected NAA's purchasing department because I hadn't had any other business pending with North American since joining Oster. And I had no reason to think we were in trouble, but I should have made sure. That episode exposed poor judgment on my part and I have never allowed anything similar to happen again.

Another Oster sales episode exposes one more serious error on my part, and again the lessons learned are valuable to entrepreneurs. If I were a private eye, I would call this "The Case of Having Too Much Information." I have always prided myself on my "in-depth" approach to sales. I turn over every stone. For this particular potential contract, I had been working diligently for more than a year at Convair at its Pomona, California, facility. Convair, Pomona was the prime contractor for the Navy's Terrier and Tartar shipborne anti-aircraft guided missiles.

Oster already had some Convair contracts, so I was very much at home there. A little too much at home, it turns out. Convair's engineering department consisted of several hundred people and over time I worked with many of them on a variety of product applications. This particular application involved an airborne electro-mechanical package, a prototype of which had already been designed and built by Convair. But Convair had no intention of producing it in-house. It was a peachy-keen contract with large quantities, and the technical aspects were right down Oster's alley. Perfect! Moreover, Convair didn't want its own prototype design to be the final production version. A specification would be written and a new design would be supplied by the winning subcontractor. As usual, it was my job to see that Oster's capabilities and off-the-shelf hardware had a strong presence in that forthcoming specification.

It was verbally emphasized by my engineering contacts at Convair that they wanted a "solid-state"—transistorized—amplifier in this device, not a vacuum tube amplifier. I thought it a bit strange since the bird already had several hundred bottles—vacuum tubes—in it, but who was I to argue? We were capable of supplying either one, but truthfully we, too, liked the solid-state idea better. Then a strange thing happened. One of my best engineering buddies was very upset one day at lunch and confided that one of my competitor's sales engineers had told him, "I'll do anything short of putting a new car in your driveway to get this contract."

My friend was so distraught that he had lost his appetite, which for him was a first. He asked me what he should do. I told him that I thought it was just a tongue-in-cheek remark by a young salesman trying to convey how much he wanted the contract. Even I could understand that. I advised him to forget it and say nothing to anyone other than his own boss. However, unbeknownst to me, he not only told his boss but also someone higher-up in purchasing. He was nervous: He didn't want to get caught in the middle.

Shortly thereafter the specifications were completed and approved and came out for bid. There were nine bidders. Oster made its bid proposal and submitted it on time along with everyone else. Then came the shocker. The low bidder was the company represented by the sales engineer who had made the remark about the car in the driveway—and his bid was for a package powered with a vacuum tube amplifier, not solid-state. After all of the engineers' verbal admonitions about not wanting vacuum tubes, for some reason they allowed the specification to be written so loosely that a vacuum tube unit would have to be acceptable if it met specs—and if it was cheaper. And it was. Vacuum tube devices were less reliable, but they were always cheaper. I could not believe Convair would accept the bid. However, since the contract had not yet been awarded, the fat lady had yet to sing.

I immediately called my reliable contact with Purchasing Liaison who was responsible for coordinating bid information between the engineering and purchasing departments. His job was to make sure everybody in both departments was on the same wave length. He and I had played golf together many times and were comfortable with each other. I told him I needed to see him "right now," so we agreed to meet after work for golf. The information I wanted concerning the bids was open information, except for prices. I wanted to know who bid what. Was Oster the only company that had failed to bid a vacuum tube amplifier? No. As it turned out, eight of the nine bidders had failed to bid vacuum tubes, and only one bidder had, which, of course, was the lowest priced bid, as it should have been.

On about the third tee, I asked him if he didn't think it odd that eight bidders who all have excellent vacuum tube capabilities bid only solid-state. He answered, yes, he thought it was very strange. I told him that all eight of us solid-state bidders were convinced that engineering wouldn't accept a vacuum tube device, and that was why none of us bid it that way. Who wants to get on the bad side of engineering? He retorted that a specification is a specification and that the bidders should have protected themselves by bidding both ways. I couldn't argue with him on that score because I already had kicked my butt around the block for failing to do just that. That was a monumental goof.

But then, on the fourth tee I dropped the bomb just as he was about to hit his drive. (In case you think me a sadistic bastard you must understand that both of us resorted to golf gamesmanship at every opportunity since we played "loser buys the martinis.") Just before he took his club away on his backswing I asked, "And what about the car in the driveway?" He dropped his club and said, "Oh shit! You know about that?" I told him, "Of course I know about that, and so does everybody else. The engineer involved didn't exactly keep it a secret. And it looks strange that the guy who made the remark works for the only bidder who submitted a vacuum tube bid, which now mysteriously turns out to be acceptable to engineering and management."

When he asked if I was going to raise a stink about it, I said, "Of course not." I explained that in my opinion it was a harmless remark, although in poor taste, made by a young—I knew the guy—sales engineer who was overzealous in his enthusi-asm for getting such a great contract, maybe his first. But I couldn't speak for the other eight bidders, who undoubtedly knew about it, too. Somebody may get the idea that a key Con-vair engineer was bribed to influence the rest of the bidders away from bidding the vacuum tube amplifier option. No question about it, there was a black cloud hanging over the entire bid process. He asked, "Well, what the hell can we do at this point?" I said, "You should be so lucky. You've fallen into a sewer and can come out smelling like Chanel Number 5 if you get your head screwed on right." He was all ears. I went on to say, "There's a way out that will remove any legitimate complaints from all of us bidders, and will unquestionably save Convair, or our be-loved government, a bundle of money. And you may even emerge a hero."

I really had his attention now. I suggested that Convair re-bid the contract, this time with the stipulation that all nine bid-ders must submit bids for both solid-state and vacuum tube versions or be considered nonresponsive. Then and only then could Convair compare apples with apples. With just one vacu-um tube bid, there was no possible way Convair could be sure it had the lowest price.

I bet him a steak dinner that the resulting savings from a re-bid would amount to thousands of dollars over the life of the contract. He took the bet and said that he would do everything he could to convince the engineering and purchasing powers to re-bid. Two days later I got a call from him saying that it was a "go"—the new requests for quotes would be in the mail within five days. This time Oster got the contract. I was pleased to find that my engineering customers at Convair seemed to be as delighted as I was.

They knew they had made a mistake in allowing the specification to go out with the vacuum tube loophole, but when push came to shove, they couldn't justify the extra cost of insisting on solid-state when the missile was already loaded with vacuum tube-powered devices. I asked an engineer, "Why didn't you call and let us know, off-the-record, that you guys would have to accept a vacuum tube version if anybody bid it?" That would have been legitimate–but, he said, they weren't allowed any contact with us after the specification was released for bid.

By the way, my purchasing–engineering liaison buddy did buy me a steak dinner—and martinis as well. And yes, the dollar savings were huge. He was a mighty happy hero, and he got a nice salary increase on his next review.

What are the lessons here? Bid exactly to specification as released by purchasing for a starter. That I hadn't was my fault. True, I was in a bind knowing what engineering wanted, but a spec is a spec. The stakes were too high to allow relationships to get in the way. And if engineering wanted to be sure of getting a solid-state package they should have clearly limited the specification to solid-state. Another lesson is to never rely on a single source or department for your information, no matter how close you may be to some of the players. Had I made an effort to quietly contact purchasing management at Convair, I most likely could have learned that a vacuum tube device would be acceptable. And the final lesson? Careless remarks, no matter how innocent, can be costly. I was very fortunate to have saved that contract.

Unexpected Opportunity

Another favorite client during my time with Oster was Convair, San Diego, the giant aircraft and ballistic missile company. Atlas missiles were born and produced in Convair's Astronautics Division where one of my most respected customers, Arthur Kuriloff, was a project manager. We didn't get a lot of business from Kuriloff's group but what we did get was very profitable, and with a minimum amount of grief.

The first occasion I had to do business with him was when he got behind the eight ball because his engineers had decided at the last minute that they needed some special, exotic DC electric gear motors in their antenna drive systems. These sorts of fire drills happened with regularity. Special motors were second nature to us because Oster probably made more electric motors than anybody in the world for its enormous variety of commercial and household products, not to mention a complete line of high-tech servos, synchros, resolvers, and motor-tach generators. But in this case the time frame was a real stinker. So I told Kuriloff right up front that it was going to cost him an arm and a leg because of the short delivery schedule. The motors would have to be built in our prototype model shop: engineering rates plus overtime.

Somehow he got the "emergency" purchase requisition approved and gave me an order without going out for bid, which saved tons of time. Oster delivered right on schedule and passed all performance tests, and I was Kuriloff's fair-haired boy from that time on. Why was this isolated incident so important to my future as an entrepreneur? That relationship unexpectedly paved the way for the next phase of my life in technical sales, which was *marketing*. Marketing and market research are two adjuncts to sales that most salesmen and their managers are never lucky enough to get exposed to, especially while being handsomely paid to learn.

CHAPTER THREE
PURE MARKETING

About a year after Oster and I had saved the day with our quick action, I got a call from my old Convair, San Diego customer, Art Kuriloff, announcing that he was now a vice president with Non-Linear Systems, Inc. of Del Mar, California. NLS was an aggressive high-tech company credited with having invented automated analog-to-digital (A-to-D) converters, a significant technical milestone that is part of almost everything we own today. These instruments were more commonly referred to as digital voltmeters (DVMs). Used to their fullest potential, however, they are much more than that. Computers cannot compute until analog data is digitized. A-to-D converters were one of the most valuable peripheral tools supporting mainframe digital computers. The emphasis was more and more on speed, that is, how many digital samples per second of analog data the converters could make; this, along with the number of data bits, was directly related to reproduction accuracy. At that time NLS was the undisputed leader.

Kuriloff said he had recommended me for a new regional
managership at NLS that was opening up in the southern portion of the U.S. As a favor to him, he asked that I consider being
interviewed for the job. This caught me by surprise because I
hadn't considered leaving Oster, even though it was beginning
to appear that both Bob Oster and John Oster, Jr. had become
disenchanted with their Sunbeam relationship.

More out of respect for Art Kuriloff than anything else I
agreed to go ahead and be interviewed. To tell the truth, there
was some degree of curiosity on my part: I wanted to see if I
could still make it through a tough interview. The worst that
could happen would be a bruised ego, which is not as bad as
losing an order. Nothing is as bad as losing an order. I had no
idea what to expect, and I had no knowledge of NLS's management structure. I had never encountered them in the marketplace, since we didn't compete, but I was aware of their products
and their position in the industry.

It was some interview. It took place on a Saturday and it
took all day. There was Andy Kay, the owner–president, and
his six vice presidents, who collectively made up his brain trust
or "Executive Council." They operated NLS as a master group.
I found myself alternately parrying questions from all seven of
them.

This was another family-owned company and, like Oster,
NLS employees were anxiously awaiting Kay's decision to go
public. Stock underwriters were beating a path to his front door,
and, according to rumor, Lazard Freres & Co. had the inside
track. The consensus among the management team was that
the company would indeed go public within the next year. It

seemed to me I had heard that song before. Yet somehow the
prospect didn't excite me and had no bearing on whether I
would take the job, if offered. The regional managership would
entail taking over the district offices in Phoenix, Houston, New
Orleans, and Huntsville, and establishing a regional headquarters in Dallas, where I would live. The salary and benefits represented a 50 percent increase over what I was making, plus a
new Lincoln Continental as my company car. My family and I
didn't really want to move to Dallas, and the monetary increase
alone would not have enticed me to leave Oster. But the job they
wanted done in the Gulf Coast was the opportunity of a lifetime for someone who loved trailblazing, someone who could
see the potential. However, it would be risky: No new sales would
likely be generated for twelve to eighteen months, assuming I
discovered any new market applications for existing NLS products or uncovered some new product ideas. That is a long time
to be a drain on company funds. I knew they needed new markets for their existing instruments and undeveloped skills, but I
couldn't help wondering if they had a realistic idea of how much
it could cost.

The job called for wearing two hats. They wanted this
new regional manager to ride herd on the district offices, which
were marginally profitable selling the existing product line, and
their one and only commissioned sales rep, who was selling
NLS instruments to aerospace customers in the Dallas–Ft. Worth
district. However, the main thrust would be to establish NLS in
the oil, gas, chemical, and petrochemical markets that dominate the Gulf Coast. That meant new markets for NLS's existing instruments, and selling its yet-to-be-identified technical

expertise to develop new products for existing markets. This would be a bona fide exciting *marketing* expedition.

Because the aerospace industry is so cyclical, I had wondered from time to time if I should consider broadening my base by adding another market dimension to my selling experience. I loved aerospace sales more than anything, but the dry spells between contracts could be frustrating. This NLS opportunity was even better than just selling different products in different markets: It would be a pure marketing exercise with sales to follow. It meant spearheading new products and services for established markets, and uncovering new markets for existing products and undeveloped company skills.

I was excited by the challenge. But on the negative side, from past experience I could well imagine the inertia that would have to be overcome, meaning the inevitable resistance from the NLS home-office establishment. Even though the company would be sending me down south to find new markets, I knew I would be fought tooth and nail if someone's comfort zone was threatened. That turned out to be more prophetic than I had imagined with respect to one Executive Council vice president who was also the sales V.P. He proved to be the most negative of the lot—and sales guys are supposed to be positive. His comfort zone was selling off-the-shelf, which is a luxury we don't always have, at least not forever. There would be no doubt about it, with new product situations requiring added engineering costs, management's comfort zone would surely be threatened.

NLS offered me the job—and I took it. Three weeks later my family and I were moving to Dallas.

The Search

After taking some time to get acquainted with the district offices in my region and with the Dallas sales rep, I embarked on my first marketing expedition. I rigged my car with an excellent transcribing machine with tapes that could easily be mailed to my secretary in Dallas, and did my dictation—call reports—while driving. My typical routine was to leave Dallas by 3 a.m. on Monday morning and return late on Friday evening, week after week. Driving the entire Gulf Coast, plus Oklahoma and north Texas, gave me ample time to compose my call reports, which were for my own perusal, not for the home office. I would analyze them for trends and similarities among my different marketing calls. The home office would get the composite results of my discoveries if anything worthwhile surfaced. But being a true entrepreneurial enterprise, NLS management did not like receiving long-winded written reports or memos. We used the telephone almost exclusively and were one of the first companies with a WATS line.

Interestingly, I didn't worry as much as I thought I would about my lack of sales productivity. The home office knew I had an empty wagon as far as salable products. Mine was a missionary's job. I had to perfect a low-key approach to potential customers that would gain their confidence and assure them that I was there to help solve problems that they might not know they had. I needed lots of information, and I hadn't the foggiest idea at this point how NLS's capabilities might someday benefit these oil, gas, chemical, and petrochemical process industries.

I decided to make cold calls rather than try to explain what I wanted over the phone. Because almost every process industry facility was located out in the boondocks I figured someone might have compassion for me, knowing I had traveled so far, and let me talk. And they did. I was known at Oster for making cold sales calls, and I loved doing it. Frequently I would make a cold call at 5 p.m., at the end of the work day, when my competitors were headed for a local watering hole. Once in awhile I would join them later for a beer and they would razz me for working so late. Little did they know. You would be surprised how many times I scored because I was there in the late afternoon, the only time some engineers and managers could see anybody—after their own people had gone home and the phones quit ringing.

Salesmen rarely, if ever, call on Ph.D.s in physics, chemistry, or geology, but that was who I needed to talk to and learn from. They were the cream of the R&D crop, working in some of the most prestigious companies in the U.S. Frankly, I found these high-powered technical research men and women thankful for the interruption.

In technical matters I can hold my own pretty well, but in the fast company of the scientists I was interviewing I was clearly on the fringe. But somehow I managed to keep up most of the time. I would usually begin by assuring my hosts that I had nothing to sell, but that we—NLS—did have state-of-the-art skills in analog-to-digital and data logging instrumentation. And because mainframe computers were coming to the fore in the Gulf Coast process industries at that time, and in some cases were auto-operating entire plants, perhaps we could help them solve some sticky problem they had overlooked because of lack of time or resources. Then the floodgates would open. I had to devise my own version of shorthand to capture all they told me. Hours later, armed with reams of notes, I would stagger out to my car and leave. Sometimes I made two such calls in a single day.

I vividly remember one meeting with a physicist that went on for three hours, about average for these meetings, during which time I hardly said a word. He would ask me far-out questions, muse for a bit, and then answer his own questions with little or no input from me. At the end of our interview he confided that our meeting had been one of the most delightful exchanges he'd had in a long time. He needed a sounding board, and I was happy to comply. And I got a lot of good data. I think that was the first time I really appreciated the wisdom of the old adage that admonishes salesmen to "shut up and listen!"

Bingo!

What I was looking for in those research interviews was a trend. In the hundreds of pages of notes I had taken I was hoping to find more than one of these potential customers with the same, or at least similar, problem. In the fourth month of this exercise I hit pay dirt. Five companies that I had visited were laboriously digitizing their mass spectrometry data by hand. Every chemical and petrochemical company in the world had at least one mass spectrometer. Could NLS somehow automate this process using analog-to-digital converters combined with some sort of peak-picking circuitry? Intuitively I knew it could be done, but I wasn't the one to make such a technical commitment.

After weighing my options, I decided to approach Monsanto Chemical Company first because I felt very comfortable with Dr. Robert Wall, director of R&D, and his chief instrumentation engineer, my dear friend now in heaven, Ed Thomason. I told them there may be a possibility that NLS could perfect a mass spectrometer digitizer. If we were to proceed, could we dare hope that Monsanto would perform the evaluation testing of our instrument, which, of course, would take time and manpower? I was assured that Monsanto would be pleased to lead the way, as it had with so many other industry developments, and if we were successful and the selling price proved to be cost effective, then Monsanto would expect to own serial number one. I signed that promise in blood.

About now you are probably wondering what all this has to do with *the fail-proof enterprise*. A lot. I cannot state strongly enough that for your new business venture to succeed, to become formidable, you *must* understand the ins-and-outs of sales and marketing. There are no practical schools on these subjects. Universities are not equipped to teach "real world" sales or marketing. They simply don't have firsthand, nose-to-nose field experience. Reading documentaries, such as this one, that detail critical sales and marketing experiences, and attending sales executive club seminars are about the only ways aspiring entrepreneurs can anticipate what they are in for—other than hands-on experience, if they are lucky enough to get some. What I learned as a result of my personal experiences forged a major part of the foundation upon which my "fail-proof enterprise" was built.

With Monsanto agreeing to work with us on the development of a mass spec digitizer, the real fun was about to begin: I had to convince the home office to stretch its technical capabilities in a different direction. This digitizer would be classified as a "system," as opposed to an instrument, and the word "system" scares the daylights out of home office bean-counters. Engineering departments don't like anything new, either, no matter how progressive they may view themselves—unless they think of it first. Having learned that from my engineering days at North American and Northrop, I didn't waste time with written requests or phone calls. I strapped an airplane on my derriere and headed for the home office in Del Mar. There, I could romance our "special products" chief engineer first and gently lead him to the trough of positive thinking before tackling management. I had finally opened a new market—which is exactly what I had been sent down south to do. But I knew instinctively that when nut-cuttin' time came and management had to commit to diverting resources to a somewhat radical new project, buyer's remorse would likely set in.

And I was right. It was a tough sell. The best commitment I could get from the "Council" was to have our special products chief engineer join me at Monsanto to see firsthand if my elevator was going all the way to the top floor. He would also try to determine what technical problems were in store for us should we elect to develop the mass spec digitizer. This was standard procedure, and I would have done the same were the company mine.

But now that I had our best engineer on my turf, I wasn't worried. He was a bright young man, and after fooling around with Monsanto's mass spectrometer for a few hours, he declared that the job could be done. We returned to Del Mar and together convinced management to fund a prototype. (This was facilitated by potential sales projections: In the Gulf Coast region alone they were well up in the multi-millions of dollars.)

Following the prototype's installation and two trips to Monsanto for fine-tuning, the digitizer was declared a complete success, meeting everyone's highest expectations. And Monsanto did indeed purchase the prototype, which was christened serial number 0001. Most other Gulf Coast companies were quick to follow suit. For the first time my region would show a profit. All of this in the latter third of my first year.

On a Roll

During the negotiations and testing phases at Monsanto, I continued to make my rounds to a few oil and gas companies, interviewing R&D directors, looking for another trend. And, by jove, I found one: Geophysics. Every oil company in the world has a geophysics department that employs geologists whose job it is to find new oil and gas deposits. When I was a student at UCLA, I took four semesters of geology for no other reason than I found it fascinating. I never dreamed that someday I might use that knowledge as I eventually did. Were it not for the fact that I could speak "geology" with these company scientists, it would have been extremely difficult for me to pick up on what they were trying to do. Consequently, I discovered another emerging market—digitizing seismic data. I had learned that all of the major oil companies were at about the same stage in computer processing—compositing—seismic data, though each was convinced it was ahead of the others. Like "Lucky Pierre," I landed right in the middle and quickly learned to walk the tightrope.

But talk about security and secrecy! I have had top secret clearances in the aerospace industry with Uncle Sam, but I have never seen security like in the geophysical end of the oil and gas business. Had Uncle had that kind of security in the 1940s, the Russians would still be looking for their first nuclear explosion.

And here I am working with all of these companies simultaneously, each one knowing I was working with the others, trying to automate the digital processing of their seismic data, which was currently being manually digitized from analog recordings.

Around this time I bought an airplane and covered my region by air. Most of my geophysical customers lived and worked in remote areas. Far too much time was being lost by driving, and flying scheduled airlines wasn't an option. Having that airplane really increased my efficiency. And after work I would take my customers and their families for a ride. The kids loved it.

Because oil and gas exploration was being forced deeper and deeper in its search for likely deposits, the returning analog signals from seismic "shots" were very weak, often almost obliterated by the low-level electrical noise generated by the geophones (microphones) that recorded the reverberations. Proprietary computer programs were developed to cancel as much of that noise as possible.

Each oil company's geophysical laboratory had at least one mainframe computer, but it wasn't always an IBM. What the geologists needed from NLS to complete the digitizing loop was a high-speed analog-to-digital (A-to-D) converter that would feed the data to the computer through a format generator—language translator—and a digital-to-analog (D-to-A) converter coming back out of the computer after the compositing was complete. The returning analog data would then be fed into huge printers, and vertical section maps would be generated to show the submerged outcrops and salt domes. The drillers would then know where to drill.

Each one of these NLS systems would represent a large chunk of business. Although the potential quantities would not equal those of mass spectrometer digitizers, it would be highly profitable with a minimum of special engineering. My gut told me that this could lead NLS into its most lucrative business over time—if I could somehow convince the home office to develop the computer portion of the system between the A-to-D and the D-to-A converters. I envisioned a single console on casters, housing a freestanding seismic digitizer-computer. This would free up our customer's mainframe computers, which were frightfully inconvenient to operate for small tasks, and seismic work was small by mainframe standards.

I wasn't as yet a computer man per se, but from my discussions with my customers' operators I knew the computational part of the seismic job didn't require much mainframe capacity. In those days there were virtually no differences between the electronic components used in our fastest A-to-D converters and those used in IBM, Univac, or CDC mainframes. The main hookers were compatible language and software. NLS had the capability if it would only take the risk to develop a compact, special purpose computer that would, no doubt, have other applications besides seismic. Did NLS do it? No!

When I failed to get to first base with management, I continued to sell our piecemeal systems to our customers. But one day about a year later I hit a stone wall at the Shell Development Company in Houston. I had been working with them for several months and was anticipating an order any day for a seismic digitizing system of about the same complexity as we had been selling to other oil companies. I made a routine visit to Shell and found they were entertaining a proposal from a brand new company, Scientific Data Systems (SDS), to supply a single package that would do the entire seismic data job. It consisted of digitizing the analog data, computer compositing, and re-converting the composited data back to analog, all in one porta-ble package on wheels. If I hadn't been halfway expecting this, I would have been totally stunned. It was exactly what I had proposed to NLS management a year earlier.

The irony here is that not only did SDS take the entire mar-ket, with huge profits, because what they were doing was cost effective, it ended up retrofitting all the companies that had NLS systems. SDS had been in business only a short time when it was purchased by Xerox for more than $90 million (in 1964 dol-lars). It then became Xerox Data Systems (XDS). The bitter pill here was that within a few short years NLS entered the comput-er business as "Kaypro"—named for Andy Kay—in, of all things, the consumer market. That was the toughest market of all, knock-ing heads with IBM, Epson, Apple, and a bucket of others. The moral to the story is this: If you are going to invest big bucks in someone qualified to lead you into new markets, you had bet-ter be prepared to listen to that person. The seismic market, which had been in the palm of our hand, was satisfied by SDS. And it was bigger than anything Kaypro ever did. Remember that sales and marketing people are in the trenches: They know more about their markets than anyone at the home office could ever hope to know.

A Twist of Fate

After I had been working for NLS for slightly more than three years, our "sales" vice president and Executive Council mem-ber was either fired or quit, along with his favorite regional manager, who covered Southern California. The Southern California region, with its hundreds of aerospace and related high-tech customers, was the number one producer for NLS. I was asked to move back to California as soon as possible. Thankfully, my family and I had rented a nice house in Dallas instead of buying because we still owned our home in Southern California, which we had rented out. We were mobile, and that is very important in the sales game. We arrived back in California in March of 1964.

It was rumored that I was under consideration for the vice president's job, but in the interim they wanted me to take over Southern California, which I did. And then, out of the clear blue sky, the former sales vice president was rehired, and I found myself in a sticky situation. The ex-Los Angeles regional manager—whose place I had taken—had been the sales vice president's favorite, but apparently Andy Kay wouldn't OK his rehire. So, the V.P. and I were stuck with each other—until he could find some way to get rid of me. He couldn't fire me without approval from the Executive Council or, in lieu of that, Andy Kay. There were bad vibes between us, but there was no way he would talk about it. He simply was not capable of having an open, in-depth conversation. And there was no question that he considered me a threat.

I had been managing the Southern California region for about six weeks when there was finally no doubt in my mind that I would never be acceptable to the sales vice president. He did everything he could to make me angry and insecure, hoping I would quit. And he continued to refuse to come out in the open and tell me what the problem was. He couldn't fire me— I had majority support on the Executive Council—but he knew how to push Andy Kay's buttons. Word filtered back to me that he had concocted some sort of story about me of a behavioral nature. To this day I have no idea what it was. Andy Kay wasn't an open person either. He bought the story without ever talking to me and I was fired without a vote of the Council. I received six months' severance pay. For the first time in my life I was out of a job.

I remember wondering the next morning, as my feet hit the cold bathroom floor, how I was going to pay for my family's twenty-one meals that day, and how were we were going to exist without medical insurance. These are the things you think about when the security blanket blows away. Oh well, what the hell. Time to move on.

CHAPTER FOUR

REVELATION—A VIRGIN MARKET

Even though I was out of a job for the first time in my life, I wasn't really sweating, although perhaps I should have been. My track record was good, and I knew it. The problem for me was where—and for whom—I wanted to work. I wasn't without advice and consultation. My ex-boss from Oster, Ward Carlson, was now in the head-hunting business with one of the most prestigious executive recruiting firms in Los Angeles. (He left Oster about a year after I did.) He wanted to place me with a good company in the worst way but I told him I wanted to take a crack at it myself. So, I took another leaf out of the old Buchanan book and made a list of five high-tech companies I would be proud to work for because of the integrity of their products and services. I wrote five letters, each one to a company president, requesting an interview. Again, I had five interviews that couldn't have gone better. But no matter. I got a disappointing surprise. Every one of those five said he would be delighted to have me work for his company, but there were no openings for a *vice president* of sales or marketing at that time!

What I hadn't realized was that my experience with NLS had priced me out of the market for any job less than vice president level. As a regional manager for NLS, I was making what the vice presidents of most other high-tech companies made, but I didn't know that. I did my best to explain that I hadn't expected a vice president position, and that I wasn't seeking a job at that level. I suggested to each that certainly they must have somebody in their sales organization they would like to replace. Most companies do. I was more than willing to scale back, prove myself, and go from there. But they were having none of that. They were afraid I would up and leave when I got a better offer. I tried to tell them that I didn't work that way, that if I were looking for a V.P. level job I would go through a recruiter, and that under no circumstances did I want to leave Southern California again. But apparently they'd had negative experiences and weren't inclined to take a chance with me.

All five companies promised to keep me on file in case a V.P.'s job did open up. Hell, I could have a gray beard by that time. I got in touch with Carlson and told him the whole story. He said he would have no trouble placing me at the V.P. level with a first-rate high-tech company if I could afford to wait, and if I would be willing to relocate. I know these things take time, and time was not of the essence with me. I had saved a fair amount from my salaries at both Oster and NLS. My family and I had never lived up to our level of income. It just wasn't necessary. We always had high quality things but in moderation. I never borrowed a dime except to buy one automobile many years before and to finance our home in Southern California.

So I took my time and tried to formulate a contingency plan in case Ward Carlson couldn't find me the right job at the right company. I was just as fussy about who I would work for as any prospective employer would be about me. So I decided to look around and see if there was anything worth getting into on my own. This was a weird experience as I had never before given serious thought to working for myself.

There were a lot of flaky things out there, but, in all honesty, I was a snob. I had worked for two first-class companies and I wasn't about to lower my standards and work beneath my skill level, not to mention my dignity. And I didn't care how much money might be made. There were more scams floating around than fleas on a camel, and you would be surprised at how high the apparent technical levels of some were. High-tech con men are real beauties. I took a full month to actively investigate and was getting mighty discouraged with the so-called business opportunities. Again, I wasn't hurting financially but *there is nothing like living off savings to keep your attention.*

Ward Carlson and I talked often and began to explore the possibilities of working together to start some kind of high-tech business. Perhaps a manufacturers' rep business. We were in agreement that we didn't want to buy an established company. Why pay for someone else's hidden mistakes and headaches? We would rather make our own.

Carlson and I were on the verge of roughing out a business plan when I got an unexpected call from Jack Lipe, an old friend I had known since high school who knew I was at loose ends. He said he had come across an unusual opportunity that he was sure I would be interested in. Jack was the sales manager for the leading Orange County Ford dealership and he interfaced with lots of people. He told me about a character he had recently met, a chemical engineer, who I just had to meet. Jack was positive the guy was sitting on a keg of high-tech dynamite and he didn't know what to do with it. Jack even offered to host a cocktail party so we could get acquainted, which he did.

The Beginning

Little did I know that this fateful meeting would be the beginning of UNI-LOC, *the fail-proof enterprise.* The chemical engineer's name was Jack Horner, and he was the chief chemist for a local water treatment chemical company. Water treatment? I never heard of water treatment! To me water is what you add to scotch and what you bathe in. I rarely drink the stuff. But Horner soon made me realize that far more water is used for industrial and commercial cooling purposes than for potable purposes. And the water used in those heat-exchange processes does its best to destroy the metal pipes and tubes it flows through. Water is destined over time to reduce all metals to their original oxide state.

This is where water treatment chemistry comes into play. Horner had blended various specialty chemicals to inhibit and protect plumbing heat exchanger tubes against the corrosion that destroys them. Acid was also used to prevent the formation of its opposite enemy, carbonate scale, which plugs up tubes. If allowed to form, calcium carbonate scale will surely plug up air conditioning heat exchangers, causing expensive repairs and downtime. Water treatment chemicals are supposed to maintain that delicate balance between corrosion and scale deposits *but they must be diligently and properly applied.* The chemistry was well-known art and widely practiced, but the *control*, the proper application of those chemicals, was guesswork at its worst. Many crude attempts had been made to automate the application of water treatment chemicals but all known methods required too much human oversight, and so they failed. Janitors and maintenance people were simply not the people who should be responsible for that oversight.

Another critical parameter that proved difficult was manually controlling water hardness, its dissolved mineral content. Fresh tapwater has low mineral content, but as it is recirculated in a cooling system it gets harder—that is, higher in mineral content—every time it travels around the cooling loop. In the loop, the water picks up heat as it passes through the heat exchanger tubes; it then flows through the main piping for several hundred feet into the outside cooling tower where the water trickles down slats, giving off its heat in the form of steam as it cools. Then it goes back to the heat exchanger tubes to pick up more heat. This recirculation is continuous. And since *minerals don't evaporate* with the steam, the water gets harder and harder, heavier and heavier, with each trip. When the mineral content reaches saturation it *precipitates*, or drops out, in the form of carbonate scale, causing a heat exchanger plug-up. (If you have ever put too much sugar into a glass of iced tea and then stirred and stirred only to see a residue of undissolved sugar in the bottom of the glass, that is saturation. Precipitation. The sugar can't dissolve unless you add more liquid.)

The only way to prevent this is by bleeding-off high mineral water from time to time and replacing it with low mineral tapwater. This was done manually by opening and closing a bleed-off valve in the cooling tower basin—if and when the maintenance people remembered to do it. This task supposedly was scheduled, but it was often overlooked or postponed. If the maintenance people failed to open the bleed-off valve or apply the chemicals on any given day, as scheduled, they would make up for it by opening the valve twice as wide the next day and doubling the chemical dosage. This, of course, resulted in corrosion peaks and excessive water and chemical usage. And that was the way every major building complex in the country was handling water treatment.

In case you are wondering, water softening was, and is, way too costly. Why not just use "once-through" cooling water and eliminate recirculation problems and chemicals? There was a day when that was how it was done, but we no longer have the water to spare.

According to Horner, the water treatment game resembled the medicine shows of old. Witchcraft. As a professional he didn't like it. His chemicals could do the job of protecting cooling systems *if they got into the water* and *if they were maintained at the proper levels*. But he had no way to control that. He was at the mercy of his customers who applied the chemicals and controlled the bleed-off daily, yet he, Horner, was responsible for the results. He desperately needed a reliable system that would control chemical levels and bleed-off, one that would remove the human element from the equation. Without such an animal, he was convinced he was about to lose his biggest and best customer, *Pacific Telephone—the venerable Ma Bell.*

This got my attention. "Ma Bell" were the magic words. But in all honesty, his control problem sounded quite primitive in comparison to what I had seen and been through on the Gulf Coast. In fact, I had difficulty believing that someone somewhere hadn't already done what Horner wanted: that is, to control pH, which is acidity versus alkalinity, conductivity for bleed-off control, and corrosion inhibitor chemical level. Nothing exotic. For the record, at that time all telephone company buildings were air conditioned not so much for creature comfort as for the preservation of the millions of switches. Those switches generated a lot of heat, and when overheated, they simply quit functioning. Air conditioning and humidity control were mandatory for the computers also. If heat was allowed to build to excessive levels, everything would shut down and all the phone calls going through that trunk would have to be rerouted at great expense and with much inconvenience. Air conditioning failures were drastic and most, by far, were traced to faulty water treatment.

But still, the control problem as outlined by Horner seemed so basic I just couldn't believe it hadn't been solved. Something was screwy someplace. Conductivity and pH were old technologies, and they were central to what he wanted to do. Anyway, I told Horner I was interested in his problem and would like to know more about it. He then mentioned that he had an electronics technician friend who would be available if we needed him. But I already knew a remarkable electronics engineer with whom I would be affiliated should this lead to a conclusive venture. I had in mind my good friend and ex-customer C. Philip Cardeiro, formerly a project engineer with Lear-Siegler and chief engineer of American Electronics, who was at this time a freelance consultant. Horner then said he would be pleased to set up a meeting with the two key telephone company engineers, Dave Posen and Sid Doney, who would educate us firsthand about the phone company's water treatment problems and what they wanted done about them. Why not? There was nothing to lose, and I wanted to verify what Jack Horner had told me. Sales potential? About 250 systems for Pacific Telephone in California alone.

Confirmation

We met with Posen and Doney, who went into great detail describing their water treatment problems. Paradoxically, when considering the value of air conditioning heat exchangers and the associated piping and cooling towers, plus the horrendous costs of failures, for some strange reason water treatment carried the lowest maintenance priority with those who had been given the responsibility. These people had not been well trained in the chemical end of things and they were too often occupied with problems they considered more important. This proved typical of every large building complex we came into contact with during later years. Water treatment was just one small part of scheduled maintenance procedures for which heavy-equipment mechanics were responsible. They were well-trained employees in their other duties, but more often than not unscheduled fire drills took priority over water treatment, a task they felt could be postponed without imminent, visible catastrophe. And it often was.

The Pacific Telephone engineers made it clear they wanted a completely automated chemical and bleed-off control system that would safely dispense *sulfuric acid* for pH control and maintain pH between 6.8 and 7.0. They also wanted a conductivity controller that would continuously monitor dissolved minerals and automatically open the bleed-off water valve as required to maintain a safe level. Additionally, they wanted a dispensing device that would maintain corrosion inhibitor chemical levels between 20 and 30 parts per million. And the entire system had to be fail-safe because it would be operating unattended for at least a week at a time. Furthermore, under no circumstances would the telephone company be willing to pay R&D or development funds for such a system. It would, however, provide its engineering building facilities to be used as a test bed any time of the day or night.

Then they said that if we were successful in meeting their specifications as outlined in the meeting, and could demonstrate reliability, the phone company would give us a purchase order for at least ten systems, if our prices proved to be cost effective. This was mind-boggling when you consider that we didn't even have a company yet. The next step was to submit a written proposal confirming the specifications and our intent to submit a prototype system for extensive testing at no cost to Pacific Telephone.

Whoa! Things were moving way too fast. I told them we needed some time to think about all we had learned and to determine our capabilities to satisfy their requirements. Doney and Posen said that if we sent in a proposal, and the phone company approved it, we would receive a "no charge" purchase order authorizing us to use specific phone company facilities for the purpose of development testing. Moreover, we could count on using their personnel to provide installation and oversight services. I then stipulated there could be no time limit on development and testing as long as we were diligent. They agreed. Privately, I felt we were in "no man's land," and previous experience told me something was fishy. I was still nagged by the question that if such a system was so damned important and a new market lay in wait, why hadn't it been done by someone else?

On the drive back to Orange County we chewed to bits everything about the meeting and the probable technical obstacles visible to us at the time (considering our nonexistent experience in this end of process control). This was a far cry from digitizing existing data. Here we would have to generate our own data. However, on the plus side was the phone company itself. Nobody could hope for a better customer. And the wastewater aspect of what we would be doing would be a bonus since the federal government was beginning to make serious noises about water pollution. There was no doubt that if we could perfect a system to meet the phone company's specs, controlling toxic inhibitor chemicals at their lowest usable levels and saving water and chemicals with automated bleed-off, we would be environmental heroes. Chromate inhibitor raises hell with sewer plants. It kills friendly bugs. With tight control we could achieve corrosion-free results at 25 parts per million (ppm) levels instead of the usual 200 ppm in general use at the time. This couldn't help but give us wider acceptance in the marketplace. Every climate-controlled building in the country had this or a related problem.

Jack Horner made it clear that if I were to proceed with forming a company for the purpose of developing and selling water treatment control systems he would leave his job and join me. He said he had been dreaming of such a system for too many years and didn't want to miss out. For the first time, he could visualize achieving the kind of results he had been preaching about to his customers. And if we bombed? He said he could always get another chemistry job. I told him I had some serious thinking to do in a very short time. I hadn't had the chance to think about who else I would want with me in such an enterprise, other than Phil Cardeiro, and I hadn't yet talked seriously with him. And then there was Ward Carlson. At this stage his skills didn't fit what we needed done, but if this turned out to be worthwhile, I would bring Ward in at a later time. I didn't want to risk his money while there were so many unanswered questions, especially since he wouldn't be able to contribute his expertise until after we had a salable product.

As I said, Cardeiro and I had a lot of respect for one another, beginning when he was my Oster customer at Lear-Siegler. He was a Yale graduate who had done postgraduate studies at UCLA, and was the brightest electronics engineer I had encountered in all my sales travels, bar none. And he had good business sense, too, considering he was a guy who chased electrons, things that nobody can even see. We had become fast friends and had a lot in common. (We were hi-fi bugs in 1956 when components such as full-range amplifiers with Williamson circuits were just hitting the avant-garde market for the first time. We built our own.) And Cardeiro and I had lots of kids, too, all stair-stepped and about the same ages: I had five and he had six. We had kept in touch during my Texas years and following my return to California, and had more than once speculated whether we might end up in a venture together.

Bait Cuttin' Time

It now began to look like put-up or shut-up time. Both Cardeiro and I knew that the telephone company venture was risky considering the probability of unforeseen technical difficulties. But we also knew that from a timing standpoint—with him a free-lance consultant with no immediate contractual obligations and me unemployed—if we were ever going to take a chance, this was the time to do it. Thankfully, we both had families who were positive in their support of our ideas and aspirations. The absence of fear was remarkable.

Financially, we were both in good shape. He and his family, like mine, had been frugal. And concerning the unknown technical "challenges" that undoubtedly awaited us, we both knew there is no such thing as a bird's nest on the ground in high-tech. Opportunities exist for the risk takers, the entrepreneurs, in the many nasty, difficult, unsolved problems that are out there waiting for our imagination and persistence. But in all honesty, I have often wondered if we would have gone ahead had we had the slightest idea of what we were in for. Although I am more than thankful we did, I still cannot answer that question. But we concluded that the visible pluses outweighed the visible minuses, so we elected to give it one bloody good go.

CHAPTER FIVE
FUNDING AND START-UP

Before I get into the formation of our new company and its organization, we should revisit Non-Linear Systems because our new company's organizational structure was influenced by the NLS management model, which represented *the* entrepreneurial leading edge of its time. Marketing and sales was only part of the education I got there. NLS was a veritable college when it came to experimental management practices coupled with behavioral science, which was just coming into vogue at that time.

NLS's owner, Andy Kay, was a graduate of MIT, who in his earlier years had worked as an engineer and engineering manager. If my memory is correct, I believe he was with Bill Jack Scientific just prior to founding NLS. He was credited with inventing the analog-to-digital converter, or digital voltmeter, which was a major contribution not only to data gathering and processing but to precise voltage measurements requiring .001 to .0001 percent accuracy. But by the time I joined the company, Kay's main interest, it seemed to me, was analyzing people. He spent enormous sums of money bringing consultants onto our "campus," and, yes, there was a college atmosphere surrounding our engineering and manufacturing facilities in Del Mar. Those consultants varied from management specialists to so-called behavioral scientists. One of the more popular NLS mentors was the famed Peter Drucker, author of the best-selling book *The Practice of Management.* Lengthy conversations with Drucker were most enlightening. His favorite saying was, "The most important things in business are innovation and marketing!"

I think Andy Kay was content with his understanding of engineers, but he was fascinated with, and challenged by, sales types. He put us through psychological profile tests of the kind used by Honeywell, the one I had flunked a few years earlier. (I had since learned how to beat those tests and could give the psychologists whatever profile they or their clients were looking for.) But worse, some NLS management and salespeople were also put through "sensitivity" training, a newly emerging secular religion spearheaded, I am ashamed to say, by my alma mater, UCLA. Many of these exercises were a gigantic waste of time bordering on fraud, and we NLS guinea pigs resented it.

Because I was then living in Texas, I was spared most of this behavioral stuff. Looking back, such punishment may have been Andy's way of keeping the sales troops out in the field where we belonged.

Student of Management

Prior to joining NLS, I had taken a Harvard Business School night course. I was a real virgin in business management and the course came highly recommended. It was very interesting, and featured the famous Harvard Case Studies. We students would read about and analyze real business problems that had almost put an actual company out of business. Some firms had even been in receivership. We would examine one company at a time, then we would write our proposed solutions, outlining the steps we would take to solve the problems and put the company back on secure operational and financial footing. I soon discovered I had a knack for this game. The Human Engineering Lab tests, which had uncovered my aptitudes in foresight and analytical reasoning, were again confirmed. By a fair margin, I outscored everyone in the class, most of whom were seasoned business managers. I also learned from that course one absolute truth that I have never forgotten—and many managers never learn: We don't manage people by directing them, we manage by leadership and with their consent to be managed.

I tell you this story because from that time on I was a student of management, not so much by studying the theoretical, which changes constantly, but from firsthand observation. And I had plenty of chances to observe the Oster Company, NLS, and our customer firms. I also had the opportunity to see how most management consultants work. I remember when Oster wanted to rejuvenate the profitability of its Avionics Division, the first thing the company did was the obvious. I say obvious because it was the "cool" thing to do at that time. Management hired a well-known national consulting firm to come in and analyze the entire operation from top to bottom. Sometimes I think company presidents—Bob Oster excluded—but especially small company presidents hire consultants expecting to be praised, to be told what great little companies they have. They willingly pay dearly to be stroked. I believe Andy Kay may have fallen into that trap. Writers like Vance Packard were invited to write about NLS's management innovations for a variety of publications, *Reader's Digest* being only one, and many did.

I have always been fascinated by the widely accepted notion that companies smart enough to engineer, manufacture, and sell products successfully, often starting from scratch and patiently building their empires over time, are in reality too dumb to find out why they are not as profitable as they once were. The answers are always the same: (1) the company isn't selling enough products, or isn't selling them at high enough prices, and/or (2) manufacturing costs are too high, assuming sales prices are in line with competition, and/or (3) purchased materials costs are excessive, and/or (4) the management burden is too high. But all that aside, there is never anything wrong that increased sales at the right prices won't cure. Unfortunately, most management consultants know little or nothing about sales or marketing because they are "textbook managers." At best, they may know a little about merchandising—dot-com, the Web, and so on—but it is an unusual management consultant who can tell a company anything that isn't already history.

Getting back to Oster's consultant: As expected, the consulting firm showed where to cut some obvious costs but also recommended cutting back the workforce, electing to produce orders already "in-house" with fewer employees. Since the order backlog was probably good for a few months, short-term profitability would surely improve whether many new orders came in or not. Now here is where a consultant can perform a service, albeit a costly one, by playing the bad guy role. If manufacturing costs were indeed too high, the manufacturing manager surely knew that he might be overstaffed without being told that by a consultant. But if he lacked the energy or the courage to make hard personal choices and lay off any of his people, being able to blame it on the consultant and top management would take the monkey off his back. Perhaps the purchasing department was buying materials from their favorite suppliers rather than always going for the best prices. The purchasing manager could now blame top management and the consultant for riding herd on the buyers or laying anyone off.

Layoffs, however, do nothing to resolve the basic needs for more aggressive marketing and sales or new product development. And when these issues are finally addressed, and new purchase orders come in, and production once again begins to increase, where are the trained people who were laid off? They are all working somewhere else. Management consultants rarely can do anything to bolster product lines, engineering capabilities, or sales over the long haul. They mainly cut and trim. Only sales and marketing consultants, if there are any, might show the way into new markets for existing products or new products for existing markets.

When the consulting firm left Oster, the short-term profitability was up. The consultants had done their job and collected a handsome fee. But in my opinion, they didn't show Bob Oster anything he didn't already know or wouldn't have figured out for himself well ahead of any crisis.

At NLS the consulting game was different. Andy Kay was too smart to let anyone mess with his engineering or manufacturing processes even though NLS was a highly indebted company. And I'll wager there had never been a high-tech company anywhere that had better borrowing ability and cost control, essential considering Kay's spending habits. He had a great money man and the best comptroller in the business. But what he seemed to be seeking most of all was his employees' undying loyalty or love. There is an old saying he probably never heard that says, "If you want support you'd better be right. If you want loyalty, get a Labrador retriever." He wanted everyone at NLS to be happy, content, and to fit the mold, his mold. So NLS consultants were mostly involved with the theoretical aspects of behavioral manipulation, not in the management or profitability of the company. But no matter how many consultants visited NLS, either voluntarily to study this radical model of management, or those on paid assignment, we salespeople remained Andy Kay's undying challenge. Man for man, Kay had the most aggressive technical sales force anywhere. Hewlett-Packard, IBM, Honeywell—none of them could begin to field salespeople who could compare with the creativity, the resourcefulness, or the energy level of the NLS sales force. Andy paid us more than any other company paid its salespeople in comparable markets, and he got value received. But he was destined never to understand us or change how we think, and it bothered him to no end.

Innovative Structure

Most new or smaller companies are notoriously poorly organized with no formal structure. Not so with NLS, which had the best, most innovative entrepreneurial organization in the annals of professional management. While I have criticized most of the things done at NLS along behavioral lines, that has nothing to do with its unique organizational concept. Unashamedly I admit copying the best features of the NLS operating model—though not the "Executive Council"—as the blueprint for UNI-LOC. Kay really knew and understood how his company structure protected and perpetuated the entrepreneurial nature of his enterprise, and I doubt that any of his consultants had anything to do with that, with the single exception of Peter Drucker. Consultants typically lead companies down the path to bureaucracy, and NLS was about as far from a bureaucracy as a company its size could be. I believe it could have doubled in size and still remained an efficient entrepreneurship.

While I am not convinced the NLS model would work for every growing business I am inclined to think it would for most. It was the epitome of simplicity. The most positive attribute was its short chain of command. From the top of the company to the bottom there were only three levels. No pyramid. The top layer was the Executive Council with the president and six vice presidents, all functioning on the same organizational level as a "master group," handling any and all policy and operational matters on a daily basis. They group-functioned as chief engineer, manufacturing manager, R&D manager, sales manager, finance manager, accounting manager, purchasing manager, and facilities manager all rolled into one. And while each vice president specialized in one or more of those disciplines, many routine decisions were made by all. But the big difference from the typical bureaucratic "management by consensus" style was that these men *were* top management! The buck stopped there.

The middle level consisted of the engineering team leaders, manufacturing team leaders, regional and district sales managers, inside sales expediters, the office manager, personnel and purchasing staff. At the bottom level were the product assemblers, who worked in teams determined by the family of instruments they assembled. There were dozens of different instrument variations in the NLS product line and each assembler worked only on specific ones, which became his or her area of expertise. There was no assembly line. One assembler put together an entire instrument, including circuit boards, and ran the final tests. Also on the bottom level were the electronic technicians who worked for specific engineering team leaders, as well as secretarial, stenographic, and maintenance personnel.

The exceptional thing about such an organization is that company growth is horizontal, not vertical. Growth at NLS was gradual and mostly at the bottom level, with more limited growth at the middle level. Middle-level team leaders could easily handle many people at the bottom level. And of course, there was zero growth at the top level, the Executive Council.

But the real beauty of the structure was the absence of the traditional "middle management" and all its attendant perks, trappings, and wet nurses. In an entrepreneurship, middle management is to be avoided at all costs. With the NLS style of management, and later UNI-LOC's as well, the *only* limiting factor to remaining an entrepreneurial enterprise was top management itself. How long could the president and vice presidents continue to personally supervise all of the most important day-to-day functions before having to resort to the middle management pyramid, the birth of the bureaucracy? To my knowledge, NLS never grew to where it had to address that question.

Even though it would be a long time before UNI-LOC would need a formal organization, I was determined to have one in place. I intended to "borrow" from Andy Kay's management philosophy to whatever degree would serve our purposes. There was no question in my mind that I would do everything possible to remain an entrepreneur for as long as I could. That would mean wearing several hats and working much harder than in a bureaucracy, but it would be well worth it to perpetuate the newly discovered ownership of my own soul!

Hard Choices

When launching UNI-LOC, I had already decided I would not go ahead without Phil Cardeiro, phone company or no phone company. But I wasn't yet sure about Jack Horner. I needed a known, proven quantity in electronic engineering and Cardeiro was it. Horner, however, was too new and an unknown quantity outside of his credentials as a chemical engineer and as the telephone company's favorite water treatment guru. Also, there was the question of money, as there always is. We analyzed our basic personnel needs for the initial phase, which would be R&D and product development, including lots of testing. Cardeiro would handle the electronic portion of the engineering task, and I would handle the mechanical portion, if any, under his supervision. Little did we know. Neither of us had even remotely considered the probability that engineering would go much beyond marrying four readily available "on the market" instruments into an integrated system that would, it was hoped, solve the phone company's water treatment problems.

Now to bait-cuttin' time: putting together a company and making sure it is adequately funded. One way to do this is to borrow money from relatives and friends or sell shares. Like an insurance salesman, plan your work and work your friends. But in order to borrow or sell shares in a brand new venture and be honest about it, the new venture's product or service must be proven and must have some degree of market exclusivity. If it is that good, venture capitalists will climb all over each other for the chance to finance the enterprise. Of course, they will want an arm and a leg, and they will be entitled to the lion's share if they do an adequate job of funding. Sadly, inexperienced entrepreneurs invariably have overinflated ideas of what their new products or services are worth in the marketplace. This is especially true of inventors who typically demand ridiculous royalties and who have no concept of market realities. Remember the Golden Rule of Business, "The one who has the gold makes the rules."

After considerable thought and discussion, Cardeiro and I concluded there were three obvious options for financing our venture. One, I would furnish all the money and own all the stock, offering options for stock purchases to key people either from the beginning or along the way. This would mean that I would be paying salaries and expenses. The second option was to raise venture capital through the customary channels. This would have been an acceptable plan were we sure we would emerge from our R&D phase with a marketable product and some degree of exclusivity. A third option was that every member of our initial core group would contribute a proportional sum of money for stock, which would be reserved for them at the outset, and we would go from there. This, of course, would mean paying salaries out of the pooled money. I figured we would need four core members, the start-up group, and ultimately five to adequately perform all critical functions on an ongoing basis.

I rejected all three of those financing options, and settled on a method of funding that was completely different from anything I had ever seen. It would be risky because this decision could make it very difficult to recruit key partners, but it turned out to be one of the most important decisions, if not the most important decision, I would make with UNI-LOC. This innovation made it possible to sustain ourselves through the eighteen-month gestation period without outside financing or selling stock, and without any money being thrown into a pool by the other participants.

This is one of the "ten essential" cornerstones of the fail-proof enterprise. I would lend the company whatever money it needed for equipment, supplies, and operating expenses at zero interest. Each original participant would work full-time at zero salary for eighteen months in exchange for a specific stock ownership pledge now! All company earnings acquired during those eighteen months would be retained in the company treasury until we had a substantial cash reserve as determined by me.

At nineteen months we would begin paying ourselves salaries. I can hear you saying, "There's no way you could get away with that in this day and age. Things are different. People don't save money today." I've got news for you: Most people *never saved money*, at least not since the beginning of easy credit. But I wasn't interested in most people. I only wanted three or four who had been smart enough to have accumulated sufficient assets to support their families for eighteen months. Today that might mean tapping into the children's college savings or your retirement accounts, but that should be no problem if your venture is worthwhile.

Let's look at my reasoning. In the first place, promises of stock are rarely fulfilled even after years of proven service. It is surprising how selfish many entrepreneurs become after the money starts flowing in and they see how much they would be giving away in stock. Even options are rarely beneficial unless the company is publicly traded and the options are received during the earliest stages.

I wanted the ownership of UNI-LOC to be established up front, removing all negative speculation. In the second place, while unemployed I had learned that the most graphic reminder you can have about your financial affairs is to be living off your savings. When new companies throw money into a pool and then pay salaries they are only kidding themselves. Nobody likes bad news so nobody wants to talk about the finances as long as the salaries are being paid. And the money man doesn't like to be the bad guy by constantly reminding everyone of the shrinking bank account. I knew that living off savings would be the brutal reminder my partners would need to keep the seriousness of our financial situation in the forefront at all times without my having to harp on it.

Cardeiro was well enough situated to finance himself and his family for eighteen months, and his wife didn't work outside the home. Eldon Means, who was my second addition to our team, had a situation identical to Cardeiro's. I was in good enough financial shape not only to support myself and my family for eighteen months, but to lend the company sufficient money, interest-free, to buy needed test, production, and office equipment, plus cover our operating expenses. Because Cardeiro and I were frugal financial planners and had no monthly payments beyond our house mortgages, we decided we didn't want anyone in the UNI-LOC owner–management group who couldn't manage his own financial affairs well enough to sustain himself and his family for eighteen months without income or personal loans. We didn't care if their wives had to work outside the home, which two of them did, and we didn't care if second or third mortgages were taken out on their homes. I was emphatic about making no exceptions to this financial integrity criterion, no matter how promising a prospective partner might be. Tough? You bet. Only the beginning.

As a side note: When it comes to borrowing money, I am probably the last person in the world to come to for advice. I would tell you: "Don't do it!" In my entire life, I have only borrowed money twice: once in 1955 to buy a new car and again in 1958 to buy a house. My family had trained me to do without until I could pay cash. And for the record, my father, who was a stockbroker, never invested a dime in UNI-LOC—or in me. No silver spoon in my mouth. I didn't need his help, not even to get through college, thanks to the G.I. Bill and my trumpet.

The bases I wanted covered from the beginning were electronic engineering, mechanical engineering, chemical engineering, manufacturing, accounting, bookkeeping, procurement, and, of course, sales. Although I would be the president and CEO, anyone who thinks a president is necessary in a new business start-up is having delusions of grandeur. With Cardeiro, we had electronic engineering and manufacturing covered with an overlap into mechanical. I could easily handle mechanical engineering under Cardeiro's direction, general management such as it would be, and sales. Sales would call for a two-pronged thrust sometime during our first year: a local sales engineer to handle telephone company business and expand us into high-rise buildings and shopping centers, and a sales manager to assemble a national sales representative network to expand our product's reach beyond California. Even if we were successful in solving Pacific Telephone's water treatment problems, it was not automatic that Ma Bell's sister companies would break down our doors to buy systems. Rivalry being what it is between sister companies, experience told me that the other Bell companies would have to be sold just as Pacific Telephone had been. And the fact that water characteristics differ throughout the continental U.S. could dictate a variety of system requirements.

The fellow I had in mind for bookkeeping, accounting, and purchasing was my next-door neighbor, Eldon Means. My dear friend Ward Carlson could have handled this assignment, too, but he lived forty miles away; and since he was a born general manager I wanted to keep him in reserve should we survive to the point of needing one. Means was a lawyer who ran the land-lease group for Humble Oil Company—Exxon—in Los Angeles, and he had studied accounting in college. Eldon Means was a purist, a lawyer's lawyer, a graduate of the USC Law School, where he should have been a professor. But he was fed up to the gills with working for a huge bureaucracy, and he did not want his own law practice either. He was ready to find out if he was an entrepreneur. We had spent many weekends together, usually Saturday nights. Our wives were friends and our boys played together. We knew each other well and needled each other mercilessly. Means was a stoic and a born curmudgeon. He would be the ideal custodian of our meager treasury.

During this decisionmaking period, which seemed lengthy but in reality took only two or three days, I had additional meetings with Jack Horner, not only to learn about the phone company engineers' reactions to our recent meeting, but to learn more about Horner himself. He was a character and a half, but one thing was for sure—this guy could sell. With his obvious aptitude for sales, I couldn't help wondering how he ever had the patience to get through Carnegie Tech with a degree in chemical engineering, a detailed discipline. He and I had a lot in common: engineering aptitudes that didn't match our personalities. But there he was, employed as the chief chemist and consultant for a water treatment chemical company. And that in itself posed another problem. I knew there were no patents or trade secrets involved in Jack's employment as a chemist, but I nonetheless didn't want us to get crossways with his present employer. Horner, however, had a legitimate reason to bring us to the phone company. As the phone company's chemical consultant, he was about to lose them as a customer if he couldn't get a handle on correcting their chemical application problems.

Do We or Don't We?

Now that he was making overtures to join us in our new company, I have to admit I had reservations about having Horner as a partner. True, he had brought us the product idea, but there were other ways to reward him. He was a likable free spirit and a raconteur, but from personal experience I knew Jack Horner would be as difficult to handle as any salesman I ever knew. And though we didn't know it at the time, there was a serious conflict of interest between Jack's employer and us. If we were successful with continuous, accurate chemical control, we would cut chemical usage by 80 percent.

Cardeiro, Means, and I finally decided that Jack Horner could be a positive asset for UNI-LOC in several ways. We especially needed his water treatment expertise during our test and evaluation phase with the phone company. However, he felt duty-bound to protect his employer's interests with the phone company so he continued in his position; it was also a fail-safe should things not work out as planned with UNI-LOC. We all agreed. It was decided that until we could deliver a successful working prototype system that reliably met phone company specifications, Horner would continue working as a chemist and consultant for his present employer. If we succeeded in our efforts, there was no doubt that Jack Horner could be exceptionally strong in expanding our control systems sales well beyond the telephone company into existing high-rise and shopping center commercial markets. He would become our outside sales engineer for California. I would just have to find a way to manage him.

We had another meeting with the phone company engineers to review the specs again, and to let them know that we would submit a "no cost" prototype for test purposes within forty-five days. In the meantime they would prepare the engineering building's cooling system for the prototype's installation at a location selected by Jack Horner.

I decided to delay the issuance of UNI-LOC stock until I was sure we had all of the prime movers, or core management, we would likely need to build our enterprise into a rock solid little company. I also wanted Horner's employment situation cleared up before issuing stock. Following prototype testing and acceptance, it wouldn't take long to round out the management team that would see us well into the bureaucratic phase, if we got that far. I knew that what I was planning to do with our stock was another radical, risky innovation, one I am sure you will have a hard time understanding and accepting. But it proved to be one of my rare enlightened strokes. It is the second essential cornerstone of the fail-proof enterprise.

In the interest of economy, I sold my new Lincoln Continental and bought a VW Bug. Cardeiro and I rented a 750-square-foot factory bay in south Santa Ana, and the four of us got together and built custom workbenches. We moved whatever equipment we had from home that fit our office and shop needs and purchased some odds and ends to get started. It was surprising how much we collected. Eldon Means began work on incorporation papers and whatever permits were needed. Cardeiro and I began a patent search for using corrosion rate sensing in water as a fail-safe interlock, locking out chemical feeds while force-flooding a cooling system with fresh water in the event of a control system failure—which is how we got our name. The official name of our brand new company was Universal Interloc, Inc.—UNI-LOC.

Move over everybody. Here we come.

CHAPTER SIX
PRODUCT DEVELOPMENT

As I said, getting into business is easy compared to remaining in business. Without our unconventional method of funding, UNI-LOC would never have survived the complications that plagued us during the next three months. To fully appreciate UNI-LOC's survival, you need to understand what we were up against in the cooling water treatment field.

All manufacturing processes generate unwanted heat. Cooling water picks up that heat and carries it to cooling towers (outside radiators), where the heat is dissipated. The re-cooled water then takes another trip through the heat exchangers to pick up more heat. The water continuously recirculates—picking up heat and cooling off.

Cooling water treatment theory is very simple. There are three parameters to control: pH, conductivity, and corrosion inhibitor chemical.

We encounter the pH factor every day in our food, soil, swimming pools, shampoos, and soaps. In lay terms, pH is nothing more than the level of *acidity versus alkalinity*. The pH scale is 0 to 14, with 0 being highly acidic and 14 being highly caustic, or alkaline. Both extremes are bad news in cooling water. Our desired control point for cooling water is pH 7, which is neutral—neither acidic nor alkaline.

Conductivity is the ability of water to conduct a current. The higher the dissolved mineral content of the water—its hardness—the *easier* electric current flows through it. Since we can relate current flow directly to mineral content, all we have to do is apply current between two electrodes submersed in water and measure the resistance to that current flow. The name of the game with conductivity is to keep the dissolved mineral content at its highest permissible level *without* forming scale, and not prematurely bleeding-off water to waste. This saves water and chemicals, thus minimizing pollution.

It is easy to add a corrosion inhibitor chemical to cooling water if there is no concern for pollution or chemical cost. But since the inhibitors of that era were zinc-chromate, which is hostile to friendly sewer plant bugs, Pacific Telephone, like all companies, was becoming sensitive to the possibility of pollution fines. We had to find a way to control zinc-chromate inhibitor chemicals down to 25 to 30 parts per million levels as opposed to the 200 ppm then widely accepted.

While Cardeiro began a relentless search for standard, off-the-shelf instruments that we could assemble into a test-bed cooling water control system, I went ahead with preparations to file for our first patent, that of using corrosion rate sensing as a fail-safe interlock. There was nothing in the patent repository archives in Los Angeles to indicate that anyone had registered that idea as prior art, although I did find one patented corrosion rate measuring instrument that measured "quantitative" corrosion rates of metal electrodes immersed in fluids. This was far more accurate than we needed: We weren't interested in mils-per-year metal loss. We were only interested in a *sudden change* in corrosion rate. Also it was a portable instrument that couldn't be adapted for our purposes. It was obvious that for simplicity and cost containment we had to develop our own.

Cardeiro analyzed the circuitry of this patented instrument very carefully to make sure we wouldn't infringe its patent. Then he designed and built our own corrosion circuitry for use as the fail-safe interlock in the phone company's system tests. And he designed and built our conductivity circuitry, which was also quite simple. We still intended to purchase off-the-shelf analyzers to control pH and inhibitor chemical. There were three pH analyzers on the market: two were industry standards, and we expected to find a suitable colorimeter analyzer to control inhibitor chemical level. Colorimetry was not a new art, but it wasn't that commonly used either.

Reality Slowly Dawns

At about this time Jack Horner introduced us to a friend of his, a chemical engineer who also had an electronic technician background. Theodore R. Barben, II, was a higher-powered chemical engineer than Horner. He had been a math instructor at a local community college and was working for a specialty chemical company. Being Horner's friend, and knowing that Jack was desperately looking for something to control corrosion inhibitor chemicals, he had been experimenting with his own colorimeter built from Radio Shack parts. He claimed it worked well in his bathtub tests and volunteered it for use in our forthcoming proto-type cooling water control system to measure zinc-chromate levels in parts per million. I was skeptical, but I had learned long ago that in engineering you try everything.

A colorimeter is an analyzer that measures the color densi-ty of fluids. It does this by shining a light through a water sam-ple stream and measuring that light by a special color filtered sensor behind the sample stream. Because zinc-chromate inhib-itor is orange in color, and its color density proportional to its parts-per-million content, a good colorimeter would relate to a direct ppm measurement of zinc-chromate.

Cardeiro had exhausted all avenues in his attempts to locate a commercially available colorimeter that would come close to our needs. There were turbidity instruments that could visually measure particulate matter, like algae, but no colorim-eters that would reliably measure color density in water. So Car-deiro, not being a chemical engineer, was happy to meet Ted Barben and his bathtub colorimeter. Although it worked well enough under our laboratory conditions, that was still a far cry from performing to the environmental requirements of outdoor installation and continuous unattended duty. Nevertheless, we integrated it into our phone company test system. We knew our first system would be a learning experience, but little did we know how much of one.

Precise water treatment control of the kind we wanted for the phone company may have been the first known effort to "automatically" walk that tightrope between corrosion and scale using a hands-off, unattended fail-safe control. And even though it was still early in the game, things were turning out to be quite different from what Cardeiro and I had expected when we agreed to pursue this project. Although we were both experienced in dealing with the unexpected as far as engineering was concerned, we hadn't considered that out of the four analyzers we would need—pH, conductivity, colorimeter, and corrosion rate—we would have to design and build three from scratch. And we hadn't even looked at pH yet.

The most important of the three cooling water treatment parameters is pH. Remember that all large cooling water systems use sulfuric acid for pH control because of its low cost, low toxicity, and ease of handling (except for its weight). But sulfuric acid has the potential to destroy a cooling system if not precisely controlled. At the time there were three major manufacturers of pH analyzers. We looked at what all three had to offer and elected to buy the least expensive unit that we thought we would need. All used a silver-silver chloride half-cell as a reference electrode, and a special glass electrode to sense or measure the hydrogen ion directly related to acidity and alkalinity.

The game plan for pH control was to keep the level just on the acidic side of neutral (pH 7). Anything below 7 is acidic, which is corrosive; anything above 7 is scale-forming. Our job was to maintain pH between 6.8 and 7.0 using an on–off control. In other words, when the pH slowly drifted upward, as it always does in recirculating cooling water, when it hit 7.0 our pH controller would call for additional acid, which would then be pumped into the cooling water slowly, bringing the pH level down to 6.8. At that time the acid feed pump would shut off. On–off control. Between pH 6.8 and 7.0, heat exchanger corrosion was not measurable, and carbonate scale could not form either, that is, if those pesky dissolved minerals were also limited by bleed-off. Tight pH control made it possible to safely maintain those dissolved minerals at much higher levels than possible without pH control, which saves a lot of water and chemicals by reducing the amount of bleed-off.

Ted Barben began to show up at our little lab-factory more and more often. I began to get the feeling that he wanted to quit his job and join us full-time. As it was, he worked with us about four hours every night during the week and all day Saturday. Ted was twenty-seven years old, looked twenty-one, and worked like a beaver. He, too, was married, had two kids, and his wife didn't work outside the home. Theirs was a typical family of the day, with a mortgage on the house and twin Ramblers in the garage.

Barben was a big help to Cardeiro in integrating our unknown and untried instruments into a system. The four instruments were interfaced and assembled in a single large enclosure with a weatherproof door. (It was to be installed on the roof of the phone company's engineering building near the cooling tower, which slopped water over everything.) Barben was the greatest help in arraying and mounting the pH, conductivity, and colorimeter sensors—electrodes—through which sample cooling water would flow. These essentially chemical engineering devices were the heart of the system. The corrosion interlock electrode would be mounted remotely all by itself, directly into the main circulating line. Corrosion interlock and conductivity were the only two system functions we were sure would perform as planned. Cardeiro had designed them.

Following accepted test practice, each event would be continuously recorded so we would have complete data for the phone company engineers: time and duration of every acid feed, time and duration of every bleed-off, time and duration of every inhibitor chemical feed, and time and duration of every corrosion interlock. Also, pH would be recorded at its actual value. The corrosivity of the water would be recorded but not in units of measure; we would log a sudden change that could only be an increase in corrosion rate. If pH was under control, that is, between 6.8 and 7.0, and the inhibitor chemical level was under control at between 25 and 30 parts per million, the resulting corrosion rate would be as low as possible. Any change could only be an increase in corrosion rate caused by a pH control failure, overfeeding acid. Such a condition would be detected by our corrosion interlock within minutes, which would then kick in, performing its fail-safe functions and alarming the user —all before any heat exchanger damage could occur.

Now that we were ready to install our test system, that old nagging question returned. Inasmuch as we were using well-known technology with the single exception of corrosion interlock, why hadn't some other company already put together an automated cooling water control system? Why weren't such systems in wide use? Perhaps the market didn't really exist on a broad scale. Or maybe it was because that until we came along with corrosion interlock there was no way to fail-safe such a system. But I doubted that. From my NLS experiences in dealing with oil, gas, chemical, and petrochemical companies on the Gulf Coast, I knew they all used pH and conductivity extensively in many different ways. They must not have had big troubles otherwise I would have heard about it during my interviews with the R&D directors. So what was fishy here? The answer was probably obvious and we just couldn't see it. But soon enough we would. Boy, would we ever.

We delivered our test system to the phone company and the installation went very well. Posen and Doney, Pacific Telephone's engineers, had everything lined up. We waited until evening to fire up the system so that Horner and Barben could join us. We rechecked and recalibrated our instruments and put the system in full automatic control mode. It worked surprisingly well for four hours, so we decided to leave it unattended through the night, knowing that the fail-safe interlock would work if needed.

Cardeiro and I returned the following morning at 6 a.m. and found the system in "interlock," with the acid and inhibitor feeds locked out and the bleed-off valve locked open. Sometime during the night the pH meter had slowly drifted away from its control point. It had called for more and more acid to bring the pH down, when in reality it was already down. The excessive acid feeds lowered the "actual" pH to about 5.0—dangerous—when the corrosion interlock took over and overrode all other functions, forcing bleed-off. During this exercise the pH analyzer recorded a "phony" pH level of between 6.8 and 7.0, which was totally wrong. The "drift" was internal, somewhere between the electrodes and the instrument.

We did everything we could to isolate and protect the pH analyzer from electrical noise interference that we thought was the cause of the instability. There were many sources of such noise on the roof of the telephone company building.

We left our system installed for a few more days, continuing to try everything we could think of. We never left it unattended during the rest of the test period. Cardeiro and I stood nightwatch and the phone company engineers kept an eye on it during the day, recalibrating pH as necessary every three hours.

Back to Square One

We also had the chance to evaluate our bathtub colorimeter. Sorry to say it, too, was overcome with drift problems. Not only was the circuitry somewhat marginal, the sensor assembly contaminated easily and the light source was unstable. Unstable light alone would cause gradual drift away from the desired control point. Conductivity and corrosion interlock passed muster, but pH and colorimetry were disasters. Back to the drawing board. Surprisingly, the phone company engineers didn't appear to be upset or discouraged. They thought we now had a realistic idea of what we were up against and that we probably wouldn't return for awhile. We weren't sure we would be returning at all.

Cardeiro read every textbook on pH he could lay his hands on, while I called my old instrumentation buddy Ed Thomason at Monsanto, to ask if he had ever had any pH problems. "No," he said. Taken aback I asked, "Are you telling me there are pH analyzers on the market that don't drift—that are stable?" He answered, "Far from it. All pH analyzers are a royal pain in the butt, but over 25 years we instrumentation people have learned how to live with them." I asked how often they recalibrated their analyzers. "Oh, about eight times a day," he said. "We have full-time technicians all over the place who do nothing else."

I told him what we were trying to do and he advised me to include a technician with every UNI-LOC system. Then, when he finally stopped laughing, he wished us luck—especially after I mentioned that we may be forced to develop our own pH analyzer. "I doubt that you'll ever solve pH drift, but if you do, call me," Thomason said. "I'll take serial number one, just like I did with the mass spectrometer digitizer."

At last I knew why I hadn't heard anything about pH problems during my R&D interviews on the Gulf Coast. All pH analyzers were cursed with the high "impedance" phenomenon! The process industries had just learned to live with them. They had adapted. I wonder how many similar "opportunities" are out there just waiting to be uncovered. Old markets begging for innovation.

The next four weeks went at a snail's pace. Cardeiro was building a new pH meter using the highest quality solid-state input amplifier (Philbrick) he could buy, in hopes of overcoming the horrendous impedance problem created by the pH glass electrode. No pH analyzer on the market had an amplifier of this quality, but cost was no object at this point. Barben assisted Cardeiro whenever possible in the design of a new colorimeter. Finally, I had the chance to dust off my mechanical engineering skills and went to work designing a new sensor—electrode— package for our forthcoming pH and colorimeter instruments, and our newly proven conductivity instrument as well. This meant that we were now designing and developing all four analyzer instruments to be used in our control system. Nothing on the market was worth diddley-squat! Hardly what we had bargained for. None of us had ever studied this hard, not even to pass final exams.

The sensor package I designed was extremely easy to service: no tools required. All that was needed was a clean cloth to wipe out the cavities through which the sample cooling water flowed, thus assuring a clear light path for the colorimeter. We were shooting for a once per month maintenance schedule with the actual task completed in under three minutes.

In this new sensor package I also included my radical new pH reference cell, which, if it worked, would not have to be recharged with electrolyte more than once a week. Because there are no impedance or noise problems associated with reference cells I knew I was on safe ground. It was the pH *glass electrode*, the device that actually responded to changes in acidity–alkalinity, that was the culprit because glass is an insulator. And there we were, passing electrons through it, trying to get a strong enough signal to amplify and use for control purposes. What a nightmare.

Our new pH meter, the first of our own design with the exotic input amplifier, was a significant improvement over anything on the market, but it was too temperamental to trust unattended long-term, even with corrosion interlock. What good is a control system if it requires unscheduled calibration and maintenance? My new reference cell worked well but I doubted the quality of the permeable liquid junction separating the half-cell from the cooling water sample stream. Should that liquid junction contaminate and plug up, that, too, would cause pH drift. I experimented with all kinds of ceramic and permeable elements and some worked fine for awhile, but when I added minute quantities of oil or sludge to the water I would get a plug-up, blocking the conductive—wet—path into the reference cell. Cooling water systems on large buildings or shopping centers don't experience much contamination because cooling towers are almost always installed on the roof, or at least high off the ground. And cooling towers are the only place where the water is exposed to atmosphere. But even so, I wasn't comfortable with a ceramic junction because it was so unpredictable. One junction would work for a month and another for a few days, so I continued searching for the magic material.

What was Jack Horner doing for our war effort during all this? He was still working fulltime for his employer so he would join us in the evenings after dinner. We worked every night until at least 11 p.m. Horner, like Barben, would pitch in and do whatever needed doing—assembly work or planning sales attacks. Horner wasn't as versatile in chemical engineering as Barben, but his instincts in the water treatment world were second to none. He kept us well supplied with information. Being an impatient sales type, this R&D period was driving him crazy, but he understood what we were up against. He did, however, start some street rumors about what we were doing with the phone company.

Let There be Light

Among his many attributes, Cardeiro had a photographic memory for electronic component specifications. It was uncanny. He stayed abreast of every new product release in the multitude of technical magazines we received every month. Our mailbox was loaded daily with no-cost high-tech publications, and Cardeiro perused the new products sections like Sherlock Holmes with a magnifying glass. One day he was reading an article on field effect transistors (FETs), weird devices with strange characteristics that as yet had no use. Suddenly a light glowed in his eyes, and he started to rummage in a stack of papers three-feet high. Eventually he came up with the specifications for a unique FET manufactured by Union Carbide. He immediately ordered some samples, which were delivered a few days later, and, for the first time in the short life of our venture, he was really turned on. He was actually smiling. And with good reason. Our high-input impedance glass electrode problems were coming to an end.

I may be mistaken, but I am quite sure we were the first company to use field effect transistors in a marketed product. Sometime later all hi-fidelity stereo amplifiers were featuring field effect transistor front-ends. FET became a household word in home music systems, but we predated that by at least a year. What Cardeiro was able to accomplish with a subminiature FET pre-amplifier was to *pre*-amplify the glass electrode current within the electrode itself. This resulted in a signal strong enough to eliminate the nasty effects of electrical noise that had been permeating the insulated cable running between the glass electrode and the analyzer amplifier. We could now run our cable for a half mile if need be, and remotely locate our pH electrodes that far from the analyzer. We could run cable in a gutter filled with water if necessary. Or we could wrap it around fluorescent light fixtures to keep it elevated, and then plug it into the analyzer amplifier with no measurable signal degradation or drift. The pH calibration would now hold for more than a year with occasional electrode cleaning. This was truly revolutionary, and we immediately began another patent search. Again finding no prior art in the archives, we filed for a patent.

I was still working on the sticky problem of the liquid junction between the pH reference cell and the cooling water sample stream. Somewhere in the back of my mind I had seen or done something that I knew would work—if I could only remember what it was. And then it hit me. Thirty years before, I had observed a capillary phenomenon when I was building a balsa wood model airplane. I had wanted to bend a wooden member and have it hold the bend. So I steamed it, made the bend, and then clamped the wood in place until it dried and held its new shape. In the process, however, I accidentally dropped one end of another wood strip into the water and noticed how quickly the water permeated from the wet to the dry end. So I picked up our shop broom, cut a two-inch section out of the middle of the wooden handle, and barely immersed one end in a cup of water. I wanted to observe how long it would take before I saw water on the dry end. It was instantaneous. This was hard wood, but it had hundreds of absorbent capillaries.

I was hoping that a wood plug liquid junction might be the long-sought solution for our reference cell application. After all, what we really needed was an indestructible blotter. An absorber. I modified our reference cell to accommodate a 5/16" diameter wood dowel and began testing. We deliberately added oil, sludge, and every other contaminant we could think of over a period of weeks. We could not get the junction to plug up. Moreover, because of the absorbent nature of the wood plug, we could fill our reference cell with silver chloride crystals instead of liquid electrolyte. Because the wood plug would not allow sample stream water to flow into the cell, only a wet conductive path, the dissolution rate of the crystals was slow. This resulted in a full two months between replenishment intervals instead of a few days using liquid electrolyte.

We now had a complete pH instrument that should easily work for months without attention. I again headed to the patent archives and sadly discovered that someone had already used a wood liquid junction many years before, though not in a pH application. That idea was now in the public domain, which meant anyone could use it. But if we could get good patent coverage on our corrosion interlock and our FET pre-amplified pH electrode, we would be in fat city. In the meantime, we had the psychological advantage of "patents pending" displayed prominently on our system. We now had the confidence to design and build a pre-production prototype system for the phone company.

Again, it was my job as the mechanical man to package the system. I had been in the fledgling aerospace industry when it became painfully clear that electronic engineers designed terrible packages. They not only looked like the spaghetti wiring of a 1939 Philco radio, they didn't begin to meet military shock and vibration specifications. So some of us mechanical types were enticed, cajoled, or coerced into working with the electron jockeys and learning to read their circuit diagrams and hocus-pocus schematics. We then applied our mechanical wizardry to produce neat, compact, and functionally sound packages that would meet military environmental specs. Packaging the UNI-LOC system proved beyond a doubt that you never know when you may need whatever experiences you have had in your life—no matter how painful.

UNI-LOC's system would never meet military specifications—it didn't have to—but we did design a rugged package that could easily stand up to all-weather, outdoor installations and ham-handed maintenance. Our system's cabinet with its swing-open, lockable front door was adapted from those used by a local golf course sprinkler control company. I contacted the sprinkler manufacturer, and we agreed to combine cabinet orders in the future, saving us all some big bucks. We bypassed plug-in circuit boards, which were very much in vogue, in favor of neat, harnessed, rugged point-to-point wiring with easy access for testing and repairs. Cardeiro did a masterful job keeping his circuitry free of nonessential components. He could get more mileage out of less circuitry—like he could with a dollar—than any engineer I had ever seen. We used the best components available. We cut no corners. Warranty service calls caused by poor quality can break a new company as fast as anything. We were just concluding our third month of company life when the new cooling water control system was ready for installation. We were determined this time.

CHAPTER SEVEN

CHEERS, TEARS & CHEERS

The installation of our reworked cooling water control system was about the same the second time around. It went quickly, and now we were exuding confidence. We just knew we were ready for business. Over the following month of around-the-clock testing we had no failures: The system did exactly what it was supposed to do. We recorded tons of data for the phone company engineers, which they analyzed in minute detail. We had no corrosion interlocks unless we deliberately induced them for demonstration purposes. We demonstrated our prototype to a contingent of Pacific Telephone Company brass, as well as to many building superintendents. Their smiles told the story, as did engineering's projected maintenance savings by using our systems throughout the company's network. We were heroes, at least for the time being.

Pacific Telephone then formally requested a bid for ten UNI-LOC Model 3500 Cooling Water Control Systems. The company also requested that our bids include all peripheral equipment, plus installation and maintenance training. The order would be sizable and, if we got it, would put the first hay in our barn. We submitted our bid and received the order one week later. We were on our way.

That evening we invited our wives to the shop and had a badly needed, well-deserved champagne party (though not Dom Perignon). We also invited our ever-reliable machine shop friends and supporters from next door. They had produced our sensor flow cells and were supportive in every possible way.

The Bomb Drops

For the time being we could forget engineering and testing and concentrate on producing a consistently reliable product. We burned the midnight oil with all hands wearing manufacturing hats. By working Saturdays and Sundays, we delivered and installed about three systems per week. About a month after receiving that first order we were finished, except for maintenance training, which was a piece of cake since the systems required so little attention. Money was flowing into our till faster than expected because the phone company had a wonderful policy of paying within ten days of billing—and Eldon Means wasted no time with the billing. It was a sensuous feeling, almost awesome, to watch our bank account grow. Then the phone company engineers called and said another larger order was coming down the pipe. Sure enough, we got that one a few days later.

We only had the new order in hand for about a week when we were hit with a big fat lawsuit.

We were devastated. We were being sued for patent infringement by the company that held the patent on the portable corrosion measuring instrument—the one we had discovered in our patent search and decided we couldn't use. Our attorney had assured us that those patent claims were well outside the realm of what we were doing. He found it strange that no one in that company had communicated with us prior to the suit, demanding that we show them what we were doing and why we thought we weren't infringing their patent. He had never seen a patent lawsuit filed without preliminary exploration and a warning. The strangest thing was that the plaintiff's attorney wasn't a patent attorney at all: He was rather a well-known Beverly Hills general practitioner with a tiger's reputation and a movie star clientele. There had to be more to this than met the eye.

Then the other shoe dropped and the answer became clear. The plaintiff had also put Pacific Telephone on notice: If it didn't cease doing business with UNI-LOC forthwith it would also be named as a party to the lawsuit and subject to possible damages. Of course, the phone company called us right away and told us what had happened—and proceeded to suspend delivery on our latest purchase order until it could complete its own investigation. At least the order wasn't canceled outright. The Pacific Telephone spokesman said that as soon as the investigation was complete the company would be back in touch with us with a final disposition. We had no idea what the time frame would be but we figured such a serious threat would surely find its way to the top floors of the phone company building.

The mystery unfolded. It seems that the plaintiff's own instrument department manager had been invited to the phone company some weeks before we came into the picture, and well before I had met Jack Horner. He had been offered the same opportunity as we had been to supply Pacific Telephone with a cooling water control system. Jack Horner knew about this because he was the one who arranged the meeting, just as he had for us. As he readily admitted, he was looking for someone to bail him out of his water treatment problems, and the plaintiff company, which engineered and manufactured corrosion measurement instruments, was the only possibility he knew of at that time. It was a well-known specialty chemical company with a small instrument department that designed and manufactured portable corrosion measuring instruments used by research people and water treatment salesmen. The upshot of the plaintiff's manager's meeting with the phone company was that he had demanded development money, to which the phone company said, "No." Pacific Telephone engineers were emphatic that the company that supplied the cooling water control system pay for its own R&D—which UNI-LOC did. So, Horner dismissed the plaintiff company from his mind and thought no more about it—until we were sued. There is a powerful lesson here.

The reason behind the lawsuit was now obvious. The plaintiff didn't really want a patent litigation, at least not at this stage. It wanted to run us out of business in hopes of being able to re-establish itself with the phone company. It had made a terrible mistake in demanding development funds and knew it. Some overzealous young manager within the plaintiff's instrument department, probably the one who met with the phone company engineers, was now on a vendetta. I couldn't help wondering if his boss knew the truth about the blown opportunity, how they had been on the inside track. Probably not. The plaintiff company as a whole had an excellent business and technical reputation, and I couldn't reconcile that with its overly aggressive behavior with this lawsuit—especially in threatening the phone company. Hardly a way to make friends and influence people. We had no choice but to fight back. We knew it would be expensive, and it was. Our newly transfused bank account was now earmarked.

I have had many dealings with attorneys over the years, including one heavy-duty patent litigation, a seven-year business dispute with multiple depositions, a few minor battles, and numerous contracts. To this day, I have never seen a better attorney for offensive harassment than the plaintiff's attorney in the first UNI-LOC lawsuit. He knew how to keep the pressure on and he did! His operating philosophy was right out of Julius Caesar: "When you've got them by the testicles their hearts and minds will follow." There were a lot of expensive depositions. Our legal bills were mounting at a rapid rate, but we kept current. *Had we been structured like most beginning companies, paying ourselves salaries out of a pool instead of working eighteen months without salaries, we would have been buried by this lawsuit.*

Saved by the "Bell"

About two weeks after the threat to be enjoined with UNI-LOC in the lawsuit, Pacific Telephone requested that I attend an early morning meeting at its administrative headquarters. Cardeiro and I were introduced to the gentleman who was the phone company's contract patent attorney in this matter. He was also a professor of patent law at USC. He promptly told the phone company brass that while he thought the plaintiff had what appeared to be a valid patent, UNI-LOC was not infringing it. This agreed with what our own patent attorney had been telling us. It wasn't new, but it was supportive. Then came the inevitable caveat. He said that a judge, for reasons known only to judges—not engineers, might find in favor of the plaintiff. There is always that possibility in a patent litigation. The telephone company of course wanted to know what its maximum monetary damage exposure could be should it continue doing business with UNI-LOC and should a judge find in favor of the plaintiff. The attorney replied that damage exposure shouldn't amount to more than 10 percent of the combined purchased prices of the UNI-LOC systems owned by the phone company at that time. He recommended that the phone company seek indemnification for that amount from UNI-LOC. He was then excused from the meeting.

When alone, Pacific Telephone's management spokesman asked if we could indemnify his company. I said something witty like, "That would surely make the Guinness Book of Records; the world's smallest corporation indemnifying the world's largest." In truth, Ma Bell was listed as the Fortune 500's number one company in assets that year. I explained that we would love to indemnify but we didn't have the money. He then asked if we were comfortable with our system pricing. I said that our original selling price to the phone company was an educated guess, and, truthfully, it was on the low side. (Now that we had built ten systems, we had a better handle on our costs.) But we would survive and we would meet our commitments.

He then asked if we would be more comfortable with a price increase. Pacific Telephone, he said, did not want undue pressure on its suppliers, especially a new supplier; it wanted to be sure we would be around to complete our contractual obligations. I replied that we would, indeed, be more comfortable with a new arrangement. A modest increase would take the cash flow pressure off now that we would be purchasing materials in much larger quantities.

Then he said: "If you did raise your prices by say, 10 percent, couldn't you perhaps set up an indemnification fund to be kept in reserve until the lawsuit is resolved? At that time it could be used to compensate Pacific Telephone for damages if you lose and any damages are assessed, or if you win, you can use it to pay your lawyers?" I was speechless! (And today, some of my acquaintances wonder why I won't even listen to another telephone company's solicitations.) We were overwhelmed and delighted, and we set up an indemnification account, to be administered by Pacific Telephone, with 10 percent of all future and pending UNI-LOC order payments withheld in that account. After the meeting, the new orders that had been on hold were released, and we were back in business. While much relieved, we still had that pesky lawsuit to deal with.

Pull Out the Stops!

We went back to work with gusto. We had an order for more than twenty systems in hand that would carry us through the next few weeks. Except for parts costs, overhead, and the two new employees we hired, all new money would go into our lawyer-wounded bank account, which, in truth, was only about 50 percent depleted of our initial earnings. Again, we worked long hours and weekends to meet the phone company's delivery schedules. We shipped and billed as soon as the systems were complete, and we were paid in advance of installation, which was billed separately.

We badly needed a few new employees, so we put out some feelers and found two bright, highly motivated men. Leo Hendrikx had worked for Philips in his native country, the Netherlands. We trained him for field service and installation work. Pat McCarville, a young man who had just been discharged from the Marine Corps, was groomed for electronic and mechanical assembly. Over time, Hendrikx developed his activities into a valuable field service profit center, and McCarville grew with us to became our first manufacturing supervisor.

Over the next eight weeks we delivered about twenty-five systems to Pacific Telephone, and we were paid for each within ten days of billing. We bought Hendrikx a new VW van and kept him busy with installations all over Southern California. Horner and I began to concentrate on how to develop a potential market outside the telephone company. As yet, we had solicited no one else, but negative rumors about our company were already being circulated by some water treatment chemical suppliers. We didn't expect to be welcomed with open arms by chemical salesmen because our systems cut cooling water chemical usage severely, but since we didn't affect boiler chemicals or algaecide usage, all was not lost for them.

Horner finally quit his day job and joined us fulltime. He had the best connections in the industry, and now he would be pounding the pavement to expand our client base. I turned my attention to laying plans to establish a manufacturer's representative sales force in the rest of the U.S. This was a big order that would take months. Horner would cover California and

Las Vegas, which held great potential for us, calling on existing large office complexes, hotels, hospitals, universities, and shopping centers.

Ted Barben had recently been terminated because his employer felt, understandably, that our enterprise was taking Ted's mind off his day job. We would now have to make the decision of whether to include him as a UNI-LOC partner and shareholder.

Meanwhile our lawsuit continued. Throughout this period, Eldon Means, our bookkeeping/accounting/personnel/legal department, was invaluable. Even though he was a lawyer, he wanted no part in the front lines of the case. He was a behind the scenes player, and I have learned over the years that while the glory boys are out front in the courtrooms, the real heroes are the Eldon Meanses of the legal world. Besides his impeccable research, Means was a stabilizing factor. None of us had been involved in a lawsuit before and we didn't know what to expect. Mack Dalgarn, of the patent firm Fraser & Bogucki, was our official legal counsel, but Eldon Means was our principal advisor and devil's advocate. And since the typical reaction when a lawsuit is dropped on you is to call the lawyer every hour on the hour seeking hand-holding consolation—a frightfully expensive response because lawyers' stopwatches are always ticking—Eldon prevented most of that. We cried on his shoulder a lot, but he decided what was important enough to pass on to Dalgarn. This saved us a bundle.

The depositions had revealed much about us to the plaintiff, which I sensed had softened its position somewhat. I think their lawyer finally realized that we weren't the bad guys we were made out to be. Since our lawyer was a patent attorney, and not very imaginative in business strategy, I took a chance and committed a cardinal sin in the eyes of attorneys: I called the president of the plaintiff company and invited him to dinner. He accepted. As a matter of fact, he insisted that I join him at his club for dinner. I began wondering who was selling whom. After limited small talk I asked if I could tell him the history of UNI-LOC, what our intentions were, and what we envisioned as our market. I assured him that we were in no way interested in his corrosion measurement market, which was well saturated by his company. I also showed him how his corrosion instrument could be redesigned to do what ours does as a fail-safe interlock, but how there was no way we could modify ours to do what his quantitative instrument does. He had nothing to fear from us.

He agreed, then countered with the thought that should we be awarded our pending interlock patent, he would be frozen out—unable to modify and use his own instrument for a corrosion interlock. He felt this was unfair considering that he had invented corrosion rate measurement in the first place. But if UNI-LOC was found to infringe his patent, then, he said, UNI-LOC would be frozen out of its own interlock application, which wasn't fair either. I had to agree with him. This man was logical. As a Ph.D., his technical credentials spoke for themselves, but he was also a genuine entrepreneur and a professional salesman. He suggested we cross-license each other without royalties or payments of any kind.

The wheels in my head were spinning. I didn't think he had a chance in hell of getting an infringement verdict against us in patent court, and I didn't think he really wanted to risk possible invalidation of his patent there either. But he was a good poker player and had come too far to turn back. He had no idea of our financial staying power, but he knew we would rather get on with business *without* the continued distraction of the lawsuit. Out-bluffing him in that kind of a game might be a satisfying ego trip but it could be ridiculously costly in both money and wasted energy. And UNI-LOC still held one big ace in the hole. I knew if he ever had designs on our cooling water control system market he would be coming to us for pH analyzers. And that was okay. I didn't want early competition but I knew that sooner or later we would get it anyway, so it may as well come from somebody we knew and not a cut-rate operator. Besides, we might need help in further developing our market against chemical company resistance. I offered my hand and said, "Pending the approval of my partners, we have a deal!"

The lawsuit was over.

CHAPTER EIGHT
IDENTIFYING THE MARKET

With the lawsuit out of the way, I could say that we were re-turning to normal, but I'm not sure what "normal" was. The telephone company released our indemnified funds and, be-lieve it or not, the amount came close to equaling our legal bills from the beginning of the lawsuit (though not, of course, in-cluding our two patent applications). By all rights, we should be able to remain in business through the inevitable dry spell that would result because we had no way to promote our sys-tems within the water treatment community. There were no ready-made, affordable advertising vehicles that reached the lev-el of people we needed to reach in order to promote our new religion—cooling water control. We were in no-man's land, just like the phone company would have been had two of its own engineers not taken matters into their own hands.

We faced a tremendous educational task. We had to bring our potential customers up to speed and make them recognize their real water treatment problems.

Every major real estate company that owns high-rise office buildings or shopping centers has the exact same water treatment problems as the phone company had—except they are totally dependent upon their on-site maintenance supervisors and janitors for water treatment performance, if they don't have engineering departments like Pacific Telephone does. They rely on consulting mechanical engineers, the ones who designed the facility's cooling equipment in the first place, for technical guidance. And those consultants will admit they don't know anything about water treatment. Short of a catastrophe, maintenance supervisors don't have the influence to get management's attention. They have no capital budgets to speak of, so even if they recognized the need for a UNI-LOC cooling water control system, it wasn't likely most of them could convince management to buy one. They had to rock along doing things the old-fashioned way, hoping not to be faulted for the occasional heat exchanger failure. Besides they could always blame the water treatment company. Here was that virgin market we had dreamed of, and there was no readily identifiable way to reach it.

In order to crack this market we would have to reach the comptrollers who held the purse strings of those real estate conglomerates. The comptrollers would know nothing about water treatment, of course, but they understood the bottom line. At the same time we would have to reach the building superintendents, all the while fighting off the chemical suppliers. Yes, we had Pacific Telephone's testimonials to help us at the proper time, but first we had to get the attention of those who had authority over capital expenditures. Plus we had to change the mistaken, but widely held, view of the telephone company as a spoiled kid who had all the capital equipment money it could ever want. This called for a three-pronged attack.

Total Chaos

The water treatment chemical business was in disarray. Jack Horner's world was the horse's tail. Every major region in the country had five or six fly-by-night water treatment suppliers. Quasi-chemical companies in that they didn't manufacture anything, these companies simply blended and formulated readily available chemicals. Everyone knew what everyone else was doing because they all were doing essentially the same thing. Some pressed dry chemicals into briquettes that were supposed to dissolve at controlled, predictable rates, but never did. (The binder used in the briquettes was clay, which is sensitive to temperature and humidity.) Others resorted to timers and drip devices and even magnets. Yes, magnets. Talk about a carnival sideshow. Witchcraft! Customer allegiance to these commercial water treatment chemical suppliers was about twelve to eighteen months on the average: That's how it long it usually took for the site maintenance superintendents to realize that the desired results were not being achieved.

By *commercial* chemical suppliers, I am talking about those who service building complexes like offices, hotels, schools, hospitals, and shopping centers. *Industrial* complexes—factories, oil, gas, chemical plants, and the like—were serviced by huge national or regional water treatment chemical suppliers who did manufacture proprietary chemicals. They were in a much higher class, and didn't have nearly as many problems with their products and services because enormous chemical usage made it possible for the suppliers to provide adequate well-trained service personnel.

Boiler water chemicals and algaecides were supplied by the same companies that furnished cooling water chemicals, making a large building complex or shopping center account very lucrative. But, like clockwork, most building superintendents would bring a new supplier on board after about eighteen months. What caused this high mortality? No control. Lousy results! The same problem Pacific Telephone had until UNI-LOC came along. Being the professional that he was, Jack Horner wasn't going to lose the telephone company chemical account without moving heaven and earth to help his customer get positive results, even if it meant selling less corrosion inhibitor chemical because of automation. That put him in a category of his own among water treatment salesmen.

Whenever a maintenance superintendent hired a new chemical supplier the results were always better over the short term, and the superintendent would breathe a sigh of relief thinking his troubles were over. But the superintendent was the victim of a little-known scam in the water treatment business. The new chemical salesman would open his new customer's bleed-off valve to a higher rate, wasting water and chemicals but severely lowering the dissolved mineral level. Lo and behold, no more scale-up problems—for a few months. This was a strange but well-proven phenomenon. Merely changing the cooling water balance by maintaining a different mineral level would clean up minor scale residue for some unpredictable period of time. But even at this higher bleed-off rate, carbonate scale would adjust to the new environment and form again because pH wasn't being controlled. High pH is also scale-forming. It would take months before things got serious again, but in the meantime the maintenance superintendent would analyze his water bills plus his higher chemical usage and he was not happy. So he would rain all over the chemical salesman.

The chemical salesman would then reset the bleed-off rates to maintain a higher mineral level, which would reduce water and chemical usage, and that again worked favorably for a short time. All would appear to be well and good for another couple of months until either a heat exchanger scale-up would occur or a failure from corrosion. The entire sequence would take about eighteen months, with the chemical salesman knowing full well from the start that his days were numbered. He couldn't repeat the wide-open bleed-off routine because the maintenance boss was wise. So in comes another new water treatment supplier. Eventually every water treatment chemical supplier in the area would get a shot at that account, and by the time they had all failed, the odds were that a new building superintendent would be on duty and it could start all over again.

To put the problem in proper perspective, *such failures were really the fault of the building superintendents who did not make sure the chemicals were properly applied every day while maintaining controlled bleed-off rates.* Of course even with daily manual or briquette or drip chemical feed, without precise pH control, the failures would still occur, just not as often. It was a laughable, wasteful, polluting mess. Welcome to our "virgin" market.

On the other end of the water treatment spectrum were the big national and regional companies that manufactured and dispensed proprietary chemicals and had better trained personnel, often bona fide chemical engineers, like Horner, handling their accounts. Their customers were more often industrial, such as the oil, gas, chemical, and petrochemical companies and the largest manufacturing complexes, rarely building complexes or commercial accounts. Many more millions of pounds of water treatment chemicals per year are used by industrial accounts. Some are so large that water treatment companies could often afford to have one field sales engineer who would service just two or three accounts, which is why the results were superior to those in the commercial buildings market, even before UNI-LOC.

Moreover, these huge process industry customers, such as Monsanto, had their own staffs of highly trained maintenance personnel who *did* apply water treatment chemicals religiously, by the book, several times a day, manually. Control wasn't good but it was better than that of the commercial users. The three national water treatment chemical suppliers who controlled the big accounts were Betz Laboratories, Nalco Chemical, and Calgon. Nalco was also a principal supplier of tetraethyl lead to the petroleum industry, while Betz was the largest water treatment chemical company—it did nothing else. These industrial water treatment companies recognized the value of control, but they had never seen reliable automated control prior to UNI-LOC. Naturally we were looking to convert them into users of our systems.

Rabid Resistance

So now you know what we were up against. Every chemical supplier knew our system would severely cut the usage of their chemicals. They wanted "control," but not by using some stupid control system. Our cooling water systems would relegate them to the status of shippers of materials, not consultants. However, whether UNI-LOC liked it or not, the chemical suppliers still controlled the market. They had influence over their customers so when they bad-mouthed us, no question about it, it set us back, phone company testimonials or no phone company testimonials.

This being Horner's bailiwick, we decided he should concentrate his efforts on trying to convert some of the regional water treatment suppliers to the realization that UNI-LOC was a fact of life, and that with our control systems they would, for the first time, have the perfect tool with which to invade their competitors. It was far better for them to get on our control system bandwagon. True, they would sell less inhibitor chemical, but they would then have—and keep—*satisfied customers*. With UNI-LOC control, they could still be consultants to their customers about boiler water chemicals and algaecides. In spreading the word, Jack Horner was about to become the leading apostle of our new religion.

While Horner was pounding the pavement in the greater Los Angeles area, I concentrated on the beginnings of our new sales rep organization. Cardeiro and Barben were busy with system production. We were getting a dribble of new orders from the phone company, so we decided to build a dozen or so systems for stock. No question, things were slowing down. We still had a healthy bank account and we knew we had received only about 30 percent of the planned Pacific Telephone orders. The phone company was now installing our systems in remote areas on unattended switch-gear buildings. But one cannot live on telephone company bread alone. We, in essence, were starting over, but this time with a proven product and some money in the bank.

At the end of each week Horner would come in and bring us up to date on his sales exploits. He had met with all the chemical suppliers in the area and a few large real estate companies that owned high-rises and shopping centers. Additionally, and this was far and away more important, he had met with three consulting mechanical engineering firms, each with some brand new building complexes on their drawing boards. They were genuinely pleased to see Jack because they knew little or nothing about water treatment, and were weary of being at the mercy of the chemical companies. These engineers understood control but they never before had the opportunity to specify cooling water treatment systems that were in concert with sound engineering practices, and with proven reliability and results.

The outcome of these meetings was that all three firms promised to include UNI-LOC in their current new building specifications, and they let Jack write the water treatment portion of those specifications—around UNI-LOC, of course. The only downside was that the jobs wouldn't be out for bid for at least a year. But with the number of consulting engineers in California who were busy with new projects, it was obvious that we had better work that side of the street for all we were worth. The new construction purchase order pipeline was at least one year in length, so if we began filling the pipeline now we would have a locked-in, predictable flow of new orders in a year's time. No one else could offer consulting engineers the package we could, so this was worthy of a full-time effort. Since it wasn't possible to split Jack Horner in two, and I was busy planning our national sales rep effort, it was time to play our ace in the hole—The Weapon, Ted Barben.

Barben's nickname, "The Weapon," stuck with him throughout his UNI-LOC career because he wore more hats during those years than anyone else. He was always eager to tackle anything. I called Ted over and asked him how long it would take him to get his registered professional engineer's license in chemical engineering. He answered, "One day." I said, "You've got to be kidding. I've heard horror stories about guys having to sit those P.E. exams two or three times." He said, "I'll take it as soon as I can get an appointment and then we'll find out." Then he asked, "Why do you want me to get the license?" I answered, "You are about to become the most accredited sales engineer in California."

He made the appointment the following week, took the all-day exam, and passed it hands down. Ted and I immediately began full-time sales training for about two weeks, during which time I imparted as much of my NLS Gulf Coast knowledge as I could. Horner boned him up on cooling water chemical options, all of which were compatible with UNI-LOC systems. Barben was embarking on a mission similar to mine in the Gulf Coast, developing an existing market for our new product and skills, and he would be dealing with professionals as I had. I knew that with "P.E."—Professional Engineer—on his business card, Barben would have an unspoken leg-up on any competitors.

His results were outstanding right from the get-go. We had worked hard on sales strategies, and Barben was a quick study. But during his first month of calling on consulting engineering companies in Los Angeles and San Francisco it became apparent that many of them were subsidiaries of New York firms. So we decided that even though we had very limited funds for travel we should nevertheless send Barben to New York City. He hopped a red-eye special and lived in a cheap 42nd Street hotel for thirty days while he called on every mechanical consulting engineer in town. The results were excellent, not only for paving the way out west, but also because he supplied them with our water treatment specifications, which were easier to use than any others, and which were compatible with UNI-LOC control systems. It was a very fruitful trip.

Back home he began steadily filling up the new specification pipeline. Horner was making some progress with existing building owners, and he also established some loose chemical company alliances. And he rang the bell big time in Las Vegas. With their high mineral tapwater—it was so hard you could almost walk on it—those hotels were ripe for our systems. Jack broke the ice by getting an order for a Model 3500 from the Sahara hotel. This led to a steady trickle of orders from other large resorts, spilling over to include some professional buildings as well. He did walk on water in Las Vegas.

Another Innovation

Over the preceding few months we had several discussions concerning the *long-term relative* values of the various management functions within a high-tech company. I made it clear from the beginning that I would have final say on share distribution, but we still talked about it because I wanted everyone's input, which naturally would change over time as we built upon our experience. However, we first had to resolve the Ted Barben question.

Did we or did we not want him as a shareholder? This discussion went more smoothly than I had expected. Barben had simply made himself indispensable. Cardeiro, Means, Horner, and I all voted to include Barben as a UNI-LOC shareholder and as the final member of our owner–manager group, provided he agreed to participate in the eighteen-month period without salary. That was how all of us were earning our shares. We called and asked him to join us that evening. After hearing our proposal he said he would have to put his wife to work, sell one of his cars, and refinance his house—but he was glad to do it.

We then had one last discussion on share distribution, after which I announced my decision. In a technical enterprise such as ours, I rated the engineering/manufacturing and sales functions equally, with support functions such as accounting and general office management at a lower level in terms of prime-moving value to the future of a high-tech company. Being responsible for general management, marketing, and sales, and having advanced the seed money, which I would continue to do as needed, I received the largest number of shares. Considering Cardeiro, Horner, and Barben equals in the long-term—with Cardeiro responsible for engineering, R&D, and manufacturing; Horner handling direct sales with established real estate companies, water treatment companies, and consulting engineers; and Barben responsible for chemical engineering and assisting in manufacturing and R&D—each received equal shares.

Eldon Means received the least number of shares since his responsibilities were accounting, purchasing, and personnel—all very important but, in reality, support functions. And as young Mr. Barben was now doubling in sales, that would further justify his level of share ownership and would prove to be a stunning bit of cunning.

Now, hold onto your hats. You're not going to believe this. Here comes another UNI-LOC innovation that I believe had as much to do with our long-term success as anything. I gave the controlling share interest in UNI-LOC to my four partners. Collectively they could outvote me. It would take all four of them to do it, but they could if they wanted to. Why did I take such a risk? Because I figured if all four partners ever did band together and outvote me on a policy then *I must be wrong*. Of course, they couldn't take my stock away but they could fire me from active participation if they wanted to. While I had complete faith in my ability to lead these men, things can happen and maybe I would become ill, incapacitated, or go around the bend and end up in an institution. My partners needed to know that in an emergency they could take control. After all, *their lives and assets were at stake as much as mine,* and I didn't want them ever to feel trapped. For the record, during all the years I was at the helm I was never fired nor outvoted. UNI-LOC's share distribution was one of the most important of our "fail-proof" cornerstones. I would not hesitate to do it again—provided I had the same caliber of partners.

CHAPTER NINE
SALES DEVELOPMENT

In my first cross-country rep trip for UNI-LOC, I was out for two weeks taking red-eye specials from place to place and sleeping in "Big 6" motels. I had six potential sales representatives to interview, two being known quantities. NLS had fallen on harder times and had decided to replace some of its regional and district managers with commissioned sales reps, just like we were about to do. It offered its former regional and district managers the opportunity to go into business for themselves as reps, while continuing to handle NLS instruments as a product base. It was a great opportunity. Several accepted but I was only interested in two, Bob Anderson in Detroit and Bob Hocker in Dayton, Ohio. These were two of the best sales engineers I had ever known. I had worked very closely with Anderson when he was my inside sales coordinator at NLS before he went into the field as a sales engineer, and Hocker was consistently one of NLS's all-time best producers, a real professional.

The other four reps I would be interviewing were new to me but each one came well recommended: one in Houston, one in New Orleans, one in Chicago, and one in New Jersey. My biggest hurdle would be teaching them the rudiments of cooling water treatment, and that couldn't be done overnight. (There was no way I would ever find instrumentation sales reps who already knew anything about water treatment.) However, it turned out they were eager to learn, and they all liked the idea of getting involved in a brand new market. I signed up the six reps and we agreed to grow together. These were first-rate people, and the more established ones had well-qualified associates. All six remained UNI-LOC reps for many years. It was a successful trip.

My previous experiences had been with company sales forces (as opposed to commissioned outside reps). In some businesses, such as Oster's, I don't think there is any choice but to stay in-house. Working as a subcontractor to government prime contractors requires too much engineering liaison for commissioned sales reps to handle because reps carry several different product lines. It isn't uncommon for a manufacturers' rep to sell as many as ten companies' products. Potential Oster-type contracts are too big with too much lead time between sales to get the needed attention from commissioned sales reps. But with products like NLS's and UNI-LOC's, which are essentially off-the-shelf technology, commissioned reps are absolutely the best way to go. When your enterprise grows into a large bureaucracy a company sales force might be preferable. With Horner and Barben we had an in-house salesforce covering the West Coast, with Horner handling the chemical suppliers and Barben the consulting engineers. The rest of the country would be covered by regional representatives and dealers.

Getting the Lion's Share

The only problem with this plan was getting enough of the reps' selling time devoted to our products. If a rep is handling ten different product lines, a ground-breaking enterprise such as UNI-LOC could not be content with just 10 percent of his selling time—not while trailblazing something as revolutionary as cooling water control systems. And reps try to handle products that dovetail to some extent—that is, products that won't take them very far afield from their regular sales calls. Sales reps prefer to have three or four of their product lines potentially applicable to each customer call.

As I became better acquainted with our reps I found they were visited, on average, only once or twice each year by the sales managers of the other companies they represented. Knowing that good salesmen, more than anyone, are suckers for great salesmen, and that all those visiting sales managers *were* great salesmen, I concluded that I would have to visit our reps four times a year, which I did. They're only human. They are always fired up by the last sales manager who visits. So I decided to be that last guy more often than the others. When I visited our reps, we spent at least three days together making sales calls. I wanted 25 to 30 percent of their time spent on UNI-LOC, and that is what I got.

Rep sales progressed slowly, as expected. It took months before they were well enough versed in water treatment to make much progress, except with the mechanical consulting engineers in their regions. I trained them to do a pretty good Ted Barben act and they did, knowing we were going to be in bed together for the long haul. A rep must be certain of that before making a long-term commitment and devoting too much sales time to one product. All of our reps invested the required pick and shovel time into their regions and soon began filling their new construction pipelines with UNI-LOC specs. It didn't take them long to figure out that when those pipelines were full and the orders began coming out the other end, they would make some real bread. They also adjusted some of their other product lines to better suit consulting engineers so that every sales call carried more potential.

Meanwhile, back at the home office things had slowed to a crawl. We had lots of pending business but nothing was jarring loose. We now had between twelve and fifteen employees and were beginning to face that old dilemma that sooner or later spooks every company—the possibility of laying off trained people. We had passed the "no salary" period for the owners, and recently had begun to pay ourselves subsistence wages. We had the reserves to hold out for a few months, but that was running too close for me. I still had substantial cash reserves of my own for a capital infusion. And although none of us really liked the idea of seeking venture capital, with our track record that kind of money was readily available and we knew where to find it. But we felt we had come too far and made too many sacrifices to give up control of our little company, at least this early in the game.

Nonetheless, in the interest of being prepared for any eventuality, I took advantage of the slack period to make a highly detailed five-year business plan, not pie-in-the-sky, but one based on our past experience plus what we had pending. I am happy to say the only thing that business plan did was gather dust. No outsider ever saw it. But there was still a frustrating drought out there, and we had no idea how long it was going to last.

I am proud of the fact that UNI-LOC never had to lay off any employees for lack of business in all the years we owned it. And if any ever quit, they always came back. We even had four rock musicians—I use the term "musician" loosely—who had a group, a band. They would work for UNI-LOC for about a year, then they would get the itch to go on the road—walkabout—for a few months, playing every night. When they were broke and physically drained, they would come back to work. Why did we put up with such a routine? Because these were four of the brightest and best workers we ever had. Today, one of our ex-hippies owns his own thriving pH electrode company. Our concept of management wasn't to force conformity. It was to our advantage to accommodate hardworking employees in any way we could. And we always tried.

Hallelujah!

Then out of the blue, with no expectations, an interesting and most welcome thing happened. In his water treatment pursuits, Jack Horner had consulted on a couple of huge industrial installations in the greater Los Angeles area, chemical customers of Betz Laboratories. Betz was by far the largest water treatment chemical supplier in the U.S. For some reason these two accounts were in jeopardy, and Horner convinced the local Betz district manager to install a couple of UNI-LOC Model 3500s to solve the problems. Surprisingly, the Betz home office approved and purchased two of our systems; they were installed on those enormous cooling water installations at no charge to the customer. These were by far the largest cooling water installations we had ever been involved with, and our control systems worked so well that not only did Betz retain those two beautiful chemical accounts, it wanted to know if we would be willing to custom engineer and manufacture a special system for them under their own logo. Be willing? Silly question. How soon and how many?

Our Model 3500 was an integrated system, meaning that all four analyzer functions were contained in a single package. Betz wanted four separate instruments—one each for pH, colorimetery, conductivity, and corrosivity—so it could tailor each "system" to the individual requirements of its customers. I told Betz we would be pleased to submit a proposal to its home office in Philadelphia within two weeks. What a surprise! We were finally recognized by the industry leader as a player. Now the local chemical suppliers could either cease being our enemies or take gas. The choice would be theirs.

I designed a new package for Betz using its own colors and logos and the new instrument mock-ups were spiffy. All combinations of individual Betz instruments would interface with each other and mount in a standard instrument rack. Jack Horner and I hopped another red-eye special for Philadelphia and met with the Betz top brass exactly two weeks later, as promised. Betz management fell in love with our mock-ups and gave us a purchase order for a quantity of instruments that would later be assembled into different system combinations, which they would spread around the country. In fine print on the rear instrument nameplates were these lovely words: "Manufactured for Betz Laboratories, Inc. by UNI-LOC." As an aside, Betz paid its bills just as quickly as Pacific Telephone, so our minor financial crisis was over.

Dealers—Another Dimension

Soon we began receiving phone calls from just about every water treatment chemical supplier of any size in the country. They were all interested in our systems and some wanted "exclusive" selling rights. (Every time I heard that it was all I could do to keep from laughing because such a request was so utterly unrealistic.) I couldn't imagine where they had heard about us. It wasn't through advertising because we hadn't done any, and if they knew about our Betz relationship they couldn't possibly expect exclusivity. However, two excellent companies did make contact with no outlandish requests, and we entered into "dealership" arrangements with them. One was North American Mogul Products Company of Cleveland, Ohio, and the other was Bird-Archer Company of Philadelphia and San Francisco. Mogul wanted our Model 3500s customized only to the extent of Mogul colors and logo, which was no problem. Bird-Archer wanted nothing special.

Over the years, our relationships with Mogul and Bird-Archer were happy and mutually beneficial. But this did pose a sticky problem for our reps: Mogul operated all over the Midwest, overlapping some of our reps' regions, and Betz, of course, operated everywhere. These dealer relationships meant a lot more work for me, but I viewed it as the opportunity of a lifetime to merge our reps into the inner workings of water treatment. So we devised a "dealer" discount arrangement with a sliding scale based upon how many systems the water treatment dealers purchased and stocked, and we backed that discount up with a reduced sales commission to our own reps into whose regions the dealer systems were installed, payable upon installation.

The reps' back-up commissions were for installation start-up and shakedown, and for warranty back-up to whatever extent was needed to assure the performance of our systems for a period of one year. *We did not warrant chemical results, only the UNI-LOC systems.* This was the best of both worlds for our reps because they weren't responsible for making the sale, and their obligation ended with the system itself, which they were completely comfortable with. The water treatment salesmen loved the set-up because only they controlled their customers; they had responsibility for the overall chemical results but not for the control systems, which they didn't understand anyway. We made the same arrangement with Betz. Wherever Betz decided to install its custom system, one of our reps got a back-up sales commission.

How did we justify the added cost of sales with dealer discounts on top of rep back-up commissions? Good question. When all was said and done, the added cost was only about 5 percent. Our reps' sales commissions were at least 25 percent higher than industry average, which is another reason we got the lion's share of their selling time. But their back-up commissions for our dealer support were only 50 percent of their regular commissions. This meant extra money for our reps because they would never, in their normal course of doing business, make

sales calls on the same people—maintenance superintendents—
that the chemical suppliers—our dealers—would. Our own reps,
like Barben, specialized in consulting engineer specifications
where chemical suppliers rarely got in the door.

But in truth, how meaningful are inflexible cost of sales
formulas anyway except to keep bean-counters happy? Sales
objectives must be weighed individually to accommodate special situations. We could afford to pay higher rep commissions
and modest dealer discounts because we didn't have any competition. We kept our sales pricing as high as could be cost-
effectively justified *based upon our customers' return on their investments in UNI-LOC systems.* That was the only luxury we had,
and rather than hoard extra profits for ourselves, we invested
in our reps. Don't ever, ever fall into the trap of skimping on the
people in the trenches who are selling your products. They are
your life's blood!

Of course, there are different kinds of businesses. Some
businesses are *price*-sensitive while others are *volume*-sensitive.
Forget product quality or competition for a moment and consider the meat business, which is almost exclusively price-
sensitive. Meat prices change by the hour, and if you just bought
200 tons of beef at a certain price, expecting to move it the following day to your regular customers at a profit, but for some
reason your customers can't use much of it, what do you do
with it? You can't store it forever. Storage costs will eat you up.
So you sell it at a loss. You take your lumps and hope to make it
up the next time.

UNI-LOC, like almost all manufacturing enterprises, is
volume-sensitive. For example, let's say that in order to pro-

duce five Model 3500 cooling water control systems per week we needed ten employees with various skills. That didn't mean those ten were always busy building their specialized parts of those five systems. Often we had other tasks for them to perform as fill-in jobs. If we could find a way to build six systems per week with the same workforce without slave-driving anybody, but by better people-utilization and planning, the gross profit on that sixth system was 84 percent, as opposed to 25 to 30 percent on each of the first five systems. Our only out-of-pocket cost for the sixth system was for purchased parts.

That being the case, we decided that water treatment "dealer" sales orders would be treated as extra business and worked into our production schedules between regular rep and direct company sales orders—without adding people.

The moral to this story is not to be a slave to rigid formulas and ratios just because they are traditional. The kind of business you have dictates what your ratios should be, and in an entrepreneurial enterprise you can make necessary adjustments quickly as you learn. But in a large bureaucracy, changing traditionally established cost ratios within the corporate dogmatic envelope is next to impossible. Just one more advantage to the entrepreneurial enterprise—and another reason why it is desirable to preserve that status for as long as you possibly can.

A New Product for a New Market

Shortly after setting up our dealer-rep cooperative sales program I received an inquiry from Stranco, our Chicago rep, about swimming pool controls.

All public swimming pool operators are concerned about the "eye burn" complaints made by swimmers who have been in the water for some time. University and college swimming coaches are particularly unhappy about this because eye burn limits their swimmers' in-pool training time. Stranco and its competitors had tried everything to solve this difficult problem. Apparently, pool maintenance people were doing a fair job of pH control but precise chlorine control was nonexistent.

The problem is that swimmers pee in the pools. And when chlorine is trickled into a swimming pool that contains a minute level of urine, chloramine is formed, which reddens the eyes. The way to remove chloramine is to add just enough chlorine to oxidize it. This is known as "break point chlorination." In answer to Stranco's plea, UNI-LOC developed an instrument that would measure and control oxidation potential, or ORP, and that would ensure there was always adequate free chlorine available to oxidize urine. Following a brief development period, UNI-LOC's first swimming pool controller was available for test. We shipped it to Chicago where Stranco tested it on a huge municipal pool. After a few adjustments and minor modifications, the tests were highly successful. We had another new product!

Stranco gave us a purchase order for a number of swimming pool controllers for its own stock, which were customized with the Stranco logo. They wanted national exclusive rights to our pool controller, and, because of the specialized market for the product, we agreed—based upon minimum quantities per year. We had appointed Stranco our upper Midwestern rep in the first place because of its leading position in the municipal and university and college swimming pool markets. The company carried a complete line of accoutrements for the pool industry and worked regularly with mechanical consulting engineers in Chicago to get Stranco equipment specified on new pool construction. Adding UNI-LOC to its bag of tricks made great sense and, over time, Stranco filled that old pipeline with lots of UNI-LOC Model 3500 control system specifications, as well as swimming pool controller systems.

An interesting story is how Stranco got its new system into the university swimming pool market. Apparently, the company convinced one of the Big 10 swimming coaches that his team could remain in the water more than twice as long as his competitors—without eye burn—if his pool had one of our new controllers. The coach couldn't resist and somehow found the few thousand dollars to buy and install one. (Probably from some wealthy swimming team alumni.) The results were spectacular, and his team won all the marbles that year. Word leaked out—I can't imagine how—and it wasn't long before every university in the conference had ordered a Stranco pool controller.

Things were perking right along for UNI-LOC. We were growing slowly but steadily. As a matter of fact, we moved to larger quarters three times in our first four years. Poor planning? Perhaps. But entrepreneurial enterprises don't indulge in the luxury of paying excessive rent on unused space. That's for bureaucracies. In reality, each move took only took one weekend, and among the five owners we had access to plenty of cheap help.

We now had our markets well under control and our "patents pending" notices, which appeared on every system or instrument we shipped, seemed to be effective in holding off potential infringers. At this point we were about a year away from our first "interlock" patent issue. Normal pending time in those days was between three and four years for a patent to be granted, modified, or outright rejected by the patent office. Today that time runs between one and two years, but unfortunately that is not the improvement it appears to be. Today's patent office research to find prior art is cursory compared to the old days. You are much better off doing your own searches like we always did. The attitude of today's patent office seems to be "Give 'em a patent and let 'em fight it out in court." The lawyers love it!

There are two schools of thought on patents. Most applicants want their patents issued as soon as possible, thinking that the protection is much better after issue. I, however, believe that the best protection occurs while patents are pending. Why? Once a patent issues, it is in the public domain. The whole world then knows what you claimed as your invention and exactly what the patent office allowed of your claims. There is always a difference. Knowing explicitly what is allowed, a would-be infringer can then work around your claims either by avoiding them completely or avoiding them just enough to muddy the waters and make it cost-prohibitive for you to sue and risk invalidating your patent in court.

But while a patent is pending, the wannabe infringer can't know what the patent office will and won't allow in the way of claims. If he plows ahead and makes a huge investment copying your "patent pending" device, he is gambling that either you won't get a patent or, at best, you will get a weak one with limited claims. But if you happen to get a "bell-ringer," the infringer is in deep trouble, with possible treble damages.

So we at UNI-LOC did nothing to rush the patent office. We knew we didn't have much longer to wait before the corrosion interlock patent would either issue or be rejected. While our research into prior art showed nothing to worry about, patent repository records are never up-to-date, they never include the current year. If anyone had beaten us to it, it would had to have been within the year just prior to our filing. We were feeling pretty confident. We bought three new company cars—one for Horner, one for Barben, and one for general use. Our salaries as owners and management had now reached the bottom rungs of the industry average for our job classifications. But then there weren't any job descriptions that included everything each one of us did. We all did whatever needed doing and it didn't matter much what it was!

Advertising?

So far I have neglected to say anything about advertising. As both sales and marketing manager, I was also responsible for advertising. We had no advertising budget our first two years, and that was just as well. There were no affordable, ready-made publications in which to advertise our cooling water control systems and reach key people. We were reaching the commercial water treatment chemical people well enough, thanks to Horner's activities. We did produce some attractive, low-cost sales brochures that were excellent for handouts and mailings, and we did generate some mailing action, thanks to "new product" releases we managed to get published—at no cost—in whatever magazines would take them.

Slowly we were getting our story out, just not by using paid ads. We took out the occasional small ad in a few semi-local, specialized newsletters, usually to announce our presence at some little local trade show. Those did create some interest, but rarely anything beyond idle curiosity. There was no way we could afford the advertising rates for the *Instrument Society of America Journal* or *Consulting Engineer* magazine. And if we could, the *ISA Journal*, while an excellent instrumentation publication, catered mainly to the oil, gas, chemical, and petrochemical industries, which we weren't primarily servicing anyway.

So, instead of ads, I spent a lot of my time writing instruction and maintenance manuals for UNI-LOC, Betz, and Stranco systems and instruments. I also wrote several treatises on cooling water treatment as practiced using UNI-LOC control for our sales representatives. Truthfully, I don't believe we could have cost-effectively utilized an advertising budget because of the screwy nature of our marketplace, and the hand-to-mouth nature of our existence up to that time. I'm glad we didn't waste the money.

However, that was about to change as we entered phase II of UNI-LOC's exciting young life, a phase that would require lots of advertising dollars and no guesswork as to where to spend them. We were on the threshold of launching our pH analyzer as a separate *industrial* instrument, completely repackaged for the wicked environments of oil, gas, chemical, and petrochemical installations. We knew from the day we solved the pH crisis at the phone company that this time would come.

But we had to be sure we could survive a head-on collision with the big boys—the well-established pH competition that was a hundred times bigger than we. My old Gulf Coast buddies at Monsanto were about to get another surprise. Although he didn't as yet know it, Ed Thomason would soon be getting another serial number 00001.

CHAPTER TEN
THE FORMAL ORGANIZATION

Coming up on our fourth year we once again had to move to larger quarters. Only this time we would be moving into our own building. One of our best customers and most staunch supporters was the mechanical consulting firm Hugh Carter Engineering of Long Beach, California, my hometown. Carter specified UNI-LOC systems on new construction at every opportunity, and he was the first consulting engineer to do so. Carter caught on early in the game because he wanted troublefree mechanical systems and he had long ago learned that water treatment was a royal pain for his customers. That is one thing we mechanical engineers have in common—we don't like medicine shows or voodoo science.

Hugh called me one day and asked if we would be interested in a new building. He said that he and his associates had some investment funds and they had thought about us. He also said the project could be structured so that UNI-LOC would be a 10 percent owner. We jumped at the opportunity, and Carter bought a nice lot in the Irvine Industrial Complex near the

Orange County, now John Wayne, Airport. He then designed our 16,000-square-foot building, and within a few months we had a wonderful new home in one of the most prestigious business airparks in the country. By then our employee count was more than fifty people and growing.

Formalizing Our Policies

Now was the time to formalize our company structure and the organization thereof—not that we had approached the bureaucratic stage, because we hadn't. But we liked being ahead of the game and wanted to be able to predict how long we could hold out as an entrepreneurial enterprise. Borrowing the basic management structure of the NLS model, we too limited our company to three layers from top to bottom. On top were the five owner–managers, who now carried the official titles of president and vice presidents. We didn't call ourselves an "Executive Council," but we functioned like one in the areas of company policies, R&D, and expenditures. However, while we made council-like, collective decisions on policy and planning, we stayed completely out of each other's backyards in the day-to-day operations of our individual departments. This is something NLS's Andy Kay would never have done.

On the bottom organizational level were the troops—the electronic and mechanical assemblers, office personnel, the bookkeeper, expediter, stock clerks, and everyone else of a nonleadperson or supervisory nature. In the middle level were our lead people, who were responsible for supervising cells, or groups. Each group included an engineer, technician, manufacturing supervisor, or support function staff, such as personnel, payroll, or purchasing. All growth would be horizontal. We would add more bottom-level personnel to existing cells or groups, and then split them off into new cells or groups as required. *But no vertical growth—middle management—would be permitted until we could no longer function efficiently as an entrepreneurial company.*

What we didn't have were engineering or factory submanagers, a chief purchasing agent, a head office manager, a human resources director, or any other middle management titles. Lead person was as far as we would go in the "title" department. My aversion to middle management and the titles attendant to those traditional paper shuffling and memo-creating jobs stems from my studies of large, bureaucratic organizations and my observations from many years of trade shows for Oster, NLS, and later UNI-LOC. Titles lead to mischief. Give employees titles like Director of Materials or Director of Human Resources, and every trade show or conference they attend will find them with their pockets and purses stuffed with resumes, trying to parlay those titles into bigger and better jobs with fancier titles. If they don't have a title to begin with, there isn't much to parlay. UNI-LOC always paid its lead people salaries commensurate with the fancy title salaries in other companies. But their business cards simply said Purchasing Department or Personnel Department or whatever.

Another problem with middle management is that they all want to be on top; they consider other middle managers a threat. And because they are not sure they have the ability to be on top, they resort to every political trick in the book, and a few that aren't. The beautiful part about UNI-LOC's three-level management structure is that the people in the middle with the "lead" or supervisory jobs can easily see the top—and that is us, the owners. We worked side-by-side with them every day.

No amount of politics can ever get them to the owner's level, so they don't even think about it.

At about this time a new management "theory" was becoming a fad, particularly with the larger bureaucratic companies. It was called "Management By Objectives" or MBO, and it became the darling of several management consultants. Now that UNI-LOC was growing, we began to attract the attention of these opportunists. Out of courtesy to a friend who had become a staunch MBO convert, we UNI-LOC owners attended several MBO seminars. These seminars were well presented, but we could never quite figure out whose objectives the consultant was most concerned with—the employees' or management's. Objectives are not always the same. The object of MBO was to get each middle manager to make a list of what he or she thought the objectives of his or her job were—or should be. Then the management consultant would meet with each one individually, and the outcome was supposedly a clear-cut view of how to advance one's career by satisfying those objectives.

Sounds good. Probably made to order for big company bureaucracies where middle management never quite knows where the boundaries are. But what a bloody waste of time for entrepreneurs! If you have time for that kind of fun and games, your company is already in the twilight zone, you just don't know it.

As far as entrepreneurial enterprises are concerned, professional management consultants are obsessed with that point in time when the entrepreneur must delegate responsibility to others—middle managers. Consultants seem to think this is the goal. It is not. Sure, some day that may have to happen, but in the short-to-medium term, most entrepreneurships can function very efficiently if they merely define and streamline their structure like we did.

You don't need power titles to get and keep employees. Pay them well for what they do, and they will stay without titles; they will work without worrying about some stylized objectives. They won't have the time: They will be doing their jobs!

Unique Compensations

At UNI-LOC we always made sure our salary levels were on the top side of industry classifications—except one, the owners. (However, by then we were only working six days a week, not seven.) But high employee salaries aren't a substitute for management's responsibility to make sure that every employee is appreciated for what he or she does. Frederick Herzberg, a noted behavioral expert, said, "Salary is a dissatisfier." And it is. *Nobody is ever satisfied with his or her salary or with how much money he or she has.* A pay raise acts as an opiate for about a week, at which time it wears off and the employee takes the raise for granted. But it wasn't the raise that perked the employee up in the first place: It was the recognition. The employee appreciated being recognized for achievement and *for being considered worthy of the raise.* Great managers are constantly on the lookout for innovative ways to let their employees know how much they are appreciated.

This is one reason we instituted a unique salary structure for all UNI-LOC employees. We rejected the idea of time clocks. They are demeaning. No more hourly pay. We instituted a base salary level of $100 per week for forty hours, and the next higher level was a $25 per week increase—big for 1965—and so on up the ladder in $25 per week increments. Now, that was worth shooting for and the next step up was always visible to our employees. How in hell can any lead person determine that one employee is worth twenty-five cents per hour more than another employee? Can't be done. All you do is make people mad. With an increase of $25 per week on the line, our employees knew it was earned. Today, that $25 increase would amount to about $75 per week.

I didn't borrow management ideas just from NLS. I took good ideas from any place I could find them. That's getting forty years experience in forty years instead of one year's experience forty times. One of the greatest ideas I ever copied came from my old aerospace employer, Northrop Aircraft. Northrop was the only nonunion major airframe company in the country. How did it maintain that status? In addition to the regular two-week paid vacation each employee received every year, Northrop closed its shop for the entire week between Christmas and New Year: All employees received full pay for those extra five days off. I remember one Christmas season when we had ten consecutive days off—two weekends, plus the paid week in between, plus New Year's Day.

What a beautiful way to get into the Christmas spirit! We *informally* adopted that same policy "objective" at UNI-LOC, and it paid marvelous dividends in employee loyalty and output. Additionally, we instigated a profit-sharing "objective" and, profits permitting, we distributed cash bonuses to all employees just prior to the Christmas shutdown. But we did not trap ourselves with a formal written company policy that said we would always close down between Christmas and New Year's Day, or that we would always give x-number of days off with pay, or that we would always pay bonuses. Each year our decision to do one or the other or both was announced to our employees by the second week of December. What we did depended on the profits up to that point in the calendar year. But official policy or no official policy, after our third year in business, we never failed to pay bonuses and shut down between Christmas and New Year's with pay.

The reason we wouldn't make our Christmas vacation or profit-sharing objectives "formal" company policy was to protect ourselves against the possibility of unionization. We had no reason to expect a union-organizing attempt, but we were surrounded by unionized companies in the Irvine complex, which meant the threat was always there. Under no circumstances were we going to have formal company policy on those matters subject to future union negotiations. In such negotiations, unions always start bargaining from where things are, never going back to square one.

However, we did establish one formal policy—that of being a color-blind employer. We had several Mexican–Americans at UNI-LOC, and some had earned their way into our middle level as lead-persons. We were one of the first companies in Orange County to work with CORE, the Congress of Racial Equality, in hiring African-Americans. It seems strange to talk about such things these days but back then our approach was more unique than common.

Another of the many useful innovations we instituted at UNI-LOC was our office bullpen. No private offices for anyone and no "Dilbert" cubicles. I hate cubicles. We had no partitions. Our office bullpen was wide open from one end to the other, though it was sound-dampened with lots of space between desks so we didn't bother each other. Even phone conversations were easily kept private. We did have a conference room and there was one other room off the bullpen that afforded total privacy, if needed for some reason. One upside of the bullpen is that you usually know where everybody is and vice versa. No time wasted looking for key people. A wave of the hand and you can have someone's attention even, if needs be, in the middle of a phone conversation. Another side benefit was that once in awhile we would overhear conversations where wrong or obsolete information was being given and it could be immediately corrected. Communications at UNI-LOC were first-rate.

We also formalized our top management titles to better reflect the duties we managers were performing. I retained the title of president, which was used sparingly, only when someone outside the company needed assurance that he or she was dealing at the top corporate level. My other official title, and the one I used in my everyday work, was "Sales and Marketing Manager." Phil Cardeiro became "Vice President of Engineering," and we found that title to be most effective in his everyday dealings with outsiders. Jack Horner had the formal title of vice president, but he used "Field Chemical Engineer," which was a disguised sales assignment. Ted Barben was also a vice president, but he retained his "T. R. Barben II, P. E." moniker because he still spent most of his days calling on consulting engineers. In his spare time we were grooming Barben to be our future V.P. of R&D and manufacturing. All things considered, we were a versatile group and, in a pinch, each of us could cover for another—at least for a short time—in every department. This is essential in a complex entrepreneurial enterprise, and reinforces my steadfast belief in the superiority of partnerships over sole or family ownerships that attempt to get cosmic performances out of hired guns.

Sales and Marketing Management

If you budding entrepreneurs can't find one person who can handle both sales and marketing management—and you probably won't—fill the sales slot first and marketing later. The two disciplines are dichotomous, related, but in reality functionally different. Characteristically, and especially as your enterprise grows, when the sales manager and the marketing manager are two different people they will fight. And while it is a big bonus to have a marketing manager who cut his teeth in sales, you are not likely to find one because companies rarely use their best salespeople as marketing bird dogs. I have always envisioned the sales manager as the unofficial "Director of Short-Range Planning." His job is to sell what is *being produced now*. He may have a flair for market research, but odds are that neither he nor his sales staff will have the time because they gotta' sell stuff now! This is what pays the bills and funds the future and, for that reason, the sales manager must control advertising.

Ideally marketing should include both researching new markets for existing products and discovering new product opportunities for new and existing markets. I like to think of the marketing manager as the unofficial "Director of Long-Range Planning." Although engineering creates and develops new products, engineers are generally not qualified to determine what those new products should be. Markets determine that. And it is the marketing department's job to find out what the markets are saying.

Large companies often use MBAs as marketers. Those guys love to play "what if" computer games and gather more data than most companies can use. The weakness of MBAs as marketers is that most of them have never been in sales or held a line job: They have never interfaced with customers one-on-one in the field. Demographic and consumer statistical data may be helpful if your company depends on how much money governments are going to spend and for what, or if it is affected by general or specific economic forecasts. But companies should concern themselves less with data gathering and more with how to get the lion's share of the untapped markets that are always out there waiting to be discovered. I would much prefer to invest in marketing people out in the field, as I was for NLS, than to invest in any number of MBAs.

Marketing requires people-persons who will get off their phones and computers, out of their comfortable offices, and into the field. They must be able to communicate on any level, whatever level is required to pick brains. This is a research job for sales-trained persons. Marketing is not for home-office types who rely on secondhand data. And by the way, public relations belongs with top management. Image building is not part of advertising.

This is a good time to address the Internet and its role in merchandising products. Contrary to popular opinion, *the Internet is not a primary sales or marketing tool*. It is a *merchandising tool*. Going on the Internet is like walking into the superstore of all superstores and not finding a salesperson. But that's okay, because 99 times out of 100 you already know what you want and why you want it before you search the net. You are already "sold" on the product or service, what you are looking for is the best deal. The Internet doesn't "sell" you anything; it displays the merchandise and you take your choice. However, as a pure marketing tool it can be used to lure test reactions to new products or services. Once in a while you may come across a sleeper product or idea with excellent potential that, until its exposure on the Internet, has been overlooked.

Now if your new enterprise has products and services that can be showcased—merchandised—on the Internet, that need no verbal sales pitch, you are indeed fortunate. Your cost of sales will be low by comparison to most businesses. However, if your products are too involved or complicated to sell themselves, then there is one way to use the Internet as a sales tool and that is in conjunction with advertising and the telephone. Advertise your products in the appropriate publications and give your Website in the ads. Then provide as much detailed information about your products as you can on your Website, being sure to highlight your toll-free telephone number so the customer can obtain current prices and delivery information. In this way, all questions can be answered by human contact and the actual sale can be made on the phone.

On the other hand, television can also be an excellent sales tool: TV salespeople can actually show, talk about, and demonstrate the features of your product or service, and compare it to the competition. Often, TV can pre-sell a customer before he or she leaves the house to visit a showroom or does an Internet search. There are scads of new gadgets in the $19.95 to $29.95 ranges that are just ducky, but that aren't available anywhere else. I, for one, am a junkie for some of these, and I find they work as advertised more often than not. Furthermore, I am convinced that the sellers of all those gadgets make more profit from "shipping and handling" than they do from the gadgets themselves. But on the negative side, TV spots are frightfully expensive and don't generally lend themselves to use by thinly funded companies. Radio is another form of merchandising that rarely sells anything although it can be pretty good at telling us when and where to find the hottest deals.

Recapping the Formal Organization

Taken individually, our innovations may not appear to be very important. But taken collectively, I assure you that they are indeed innovative dynamite. Today I see a lot of entrepreneurships where the owners seem to consider employees only as "warm bodies" who can be trained to push color-coded buttons to produce a product. Management doesn't seem to realize that every employee is potentially a loyal, reliable, and valuable asset—if treated as a real person. Your employees will go the extra mile if you do likewise. Don't leave this to your personnel or human resources directors. All they know are textbook behavioral theories. Give me a motivated workforce and I'll skin my competition every time.

CHAPTER ELEVEN

MOVING MOUNTAINS

Phil Cardeiro and his staff had been busy for some time augmenting our product line, and we now had five different UNI-LOC cooling water control systems, all variations of the original Model 3500. We found that many of the local chemical companies, those who service smaller buildings and complexes, could only justify stripped-down models on small air conditioning systems, sometimes without corrosion interlock. The reliability and predictability of our pH instruments made this feasible. Betz Laboratories and Mogul continued selling our systems to their existing customers. All in all, we were sitting pretty well in the growing cooling water control business.

It was around that time the federal government's Department of the Interior contacted us to bid on a battery-powered portable "Water Quality Monitoring System" for installation in remote areas; its job was to sample stream and lake water and record the data for later analysis. The feds were finally getting exercised about water pollution.

The monitors were to analyze and data-record five or six water quality parameters. Of those parameters, UNI-LOC designed and manufactured only pH and conductivity instruments, in this case as related to water hardness. We would have to purchase the other three or four monitoring instruments from different manufacturers, package them into a portable weatherproof carrying case, and take full responsibility for the performance of the whole package. The order would be for a large quantity and the bid specifications went out to at least ten potential suppliers. Dollarwise this would dwarf any single order we had ever received up until that time.

However, we declined to bid, and the feds were furious. They knew we had the only pH instrument that would operate unattended and without service for months at a time, and pH was the most important system parameter to be sampled and recorded. Why did we "no-bid?" The main reason was that we didn't want to deal directly with the federal government, or with any state or local government for that matter. I learned at Oster that Uncle Sam doesn't want its suppliers to make money. (Remember the Oster F-86 actuator battle?) If you receive a government contract and you lose your shirt on it, the government could care less. It won't help except to the extent of *maybe* picking up some of your lost costs—the government didn't with Oster—but Uncle Sam won't make up any lost fixed-fee profit. However, if by being efficient you happen to make more profit than the contract fixed-fee, you have to "renegotiate" the difference and take a cut. It is a one-way street, and we would be going the wrong way. We made a firm policy when we formed UNI-LOC that we would never be a prime contractor to any government entity, except in time of war.

Another reason we "no-bid" this project was that we did not want full-package responsibility for instruments we ourselves had not designed and manufactured. Talk about a prescription for mischief! We knew we would end up hiring a cadre of field service technicians and flying them all over the country to continuously service water quality monitors for the life of the contract. We weren't worried about the two UNI-LOC instruments, but we were plenty concerned about the instruments supplied by others. We also knew that whatever company was unfortunate enough to get this contract would—unless they were crazy—be coming to us for pH analyzers. And they did. We received several requests over the next few years to bid government jobs including our pH instruments, and they were always muddied-up by costly government environmental specifications. But we stuck to our guns. We told the feds we would be happy to sell them our standard, off-the-shelf analyzers and they could make their own special packaging. And that is precisely what they did—but through third parties. They always found some desperate sucker to do it, using UNI-LOC pH analyzers and sometimes our conductivity instruments as well.

New Ball Game

But we now knew that UNI-LOC's future growth would mostly hinge upon selling our pH analyzers to the liquid process industries—oil, gas, chemical, petrochemical, and food and beverage. But to satisfy the various industries' differing requirements, we would have to produce some new models that were totally different from our water treatment pH instruments. We would need to develop compact units with all-weather enclosures, even explosion-proof enclosures for some applications. We would also need a broader variety of pH reference cell and glass electrode configurations made from inert materials. Along that line, we developed a completely submersible electrode assembly that could be thrown overboard, like a boat anchor, into a contaminated wastepond. You name it, we did it. That's the beauty of the fast moving, lean and mean entrepreneurship.

But this also meant we could no longer rely on a simple "on-off" control, as we had with cooling water pH. This was the big league. We needed "proportional" control outputs that could interface with our competitors' peripheral equipment, which had been in wide use for years. Once again, Cardeiro and his technical staff came through with a masterpiece we called our Model 1000 pH analyzer. It had outputs and installation options suitable for any application. As with our older instruments and systems, emphasis was placed on reliability and ease of maintenance in the field, meaning without tools. To force our customers to remove a UNI-LOC instrument from its installation and take it to a lab for repairs was unthinkable as far as we were concerned.

We knew our new Model 1000 was the cat's meow, but we were perplexed on how to market it. This was far different from selling our original cooling water control systems, and that had been tough enough in the beginning. Besides the telephone company, we hadn't had any ready market for cooling water control systems at all. But it was just the opposite with industrial pH analyzers. There were well-established markets all over the place, but in the persons of our competitors. We had years of bias, habit, and favoritism to overcome to get our Model 1000s installed.

We were going to compete with the two giants who had owned the industrial pH markets for twenty-five years straight.

For a novelty, we now had something of an advertising budget and we were prepared to spend it. The problem was where to begin: Which advertising vehicles should carry our initial thrust? Some magazines were aimed at the huge engineering-constructors—firms like Bechtel, Fluor, Braun, Brown & Root—the folks who design and build the big industrial process plants that were our prime targets. Other publications were aimed at the end-users—operating plants like Monsanto, Union Carbide, Texaco, and Shell. Still other magazines were aimed at the food and beverage process industries.

We couldn't begin to afford ads in all of them, although we did flood every one with "new product releases," which are free and almost as good as ads. (The only problem with that is that we could only do it once in awhile with each magazine, unless we regularly bought ad space.) The responses to our product releases were excellent. Our little one-person literature department was overwhelmed mailing out our information packets. But we still weren't ready for an ad campaign.

I wanted to get out in the field and do some hands-on market research before committing to any regular, institutional ad program. So I boxed up two Model 1000s, serial numbers 00001 and 00002, hopped a plane to Houston, and then drove to Texas City to visit Monsanto. It was like old home week. Ed Thomason said he was ready to shake down our 1000s like they would never be shaken down again. I told him to have at it. He did. If we had any weak spots in our design, now was the time to find them. In the few days I was there, Ed tested the instruments in a number of diabolical ways, and at the end of the trials, he said, "I'll get you a purchase order and a check for these. You're not getting them back. And I'll be wanting more." I guess this is what "mutual benefits" are all about.

However, when I made some cold marketing calls while in the Gulf Coast area, I found an almost indifferent response to our Model 1000. Unlike my marketing forays for NLS when I was interviewing directors of R&D, I was now dealing with instrumentation engineers and technicians in these same oil, gas, chemical, and petrochemical companies. I soon learned that not many Gulf Coast companies at that time had forward-thinking instrumentation engineers like Monsanto's Ed Thomason. And, of course, I had to accept the fact that these potential new customers didn't know me from Adam, while Ed knew me from the good old days. To this new group, I was just a guy selling pH analyzers, and one who had a bizarre, highly suspect story at that. I tried to avoid dropping Thomason's name during these calls because the Gulf Coast was one big community. The engineers and technicians all knew one another through their professional organizations. I knew that Thomason would give us great reviews, but I had to be patient and let him do it in his own time. As you have already guessed, patience isn't one of my virtues.

Shifting Gears

I returned home more frustrated than ever. I had to find a way to get this fantastic pH story in front of the right people—and make them believe it, at least to the extent of giving us a chance to prove it. Within a day or two of my return, in walks Cochrane Chase of the advertising agency Cochran Chase & Company. He was making a *cold sales call*. Chase was a personable fellow and struck me as being not only bright but as eager to learn about our marketplace as I was to learn the ad game. We began a long and rewarding relationship.

I told him that in our first real ad we wanted to shock the process industries, so together we devised a half-page ad for the *ISA Journal*—the Instrument Society of America's periodical, which is the process industry's instrumentation engineer's bible. In the ad we showed a pH glass electrode—with our built-in FET pre-amp—completely submerged in a beaker of water, electrical leads and all, and text describing how our electrodes and analyzer would function reliably, unaffected, in such an environment. The ad brought in a good response, many requests for additional information—but no orders.

All of our reps now had Model 1000 demonstrators and were making slow headway here and there, but nothing like we had anticipated. We continued to advertise modestly and always got good response, requests for literature and more engineering data. We would mail the info off and send copies of the inquiries to our reps and they would follow up; every once in a while we would get an order. Those who did take the chance and bought a 1000 were ecstatic with the results and they bought more. We were gradually breaking down the doors, but far too slowly for such a revolutionary product.

About a year later, I learned from some of our most satisfied customers that they just hadn't believed our ads and literature when we first introduced the Model 1000. They said it was too pie-in-the-sky, that they had lived with pH analyzer problems far too long to believe that anybody could leapfrog the big boys like we did. Good grief! Where does an alien go to register?

Nonetheless, our advertising in the *ISA Journal* had been effective enough, so we decided to rupture what was left of the ad budget and enter our first trade show, the ISA Show in Chicago. We hastily designed an attractive booth, portable by most standards, which could accommodate a half dozen *operating* pH analyzers in several contrived environments. It was a display that could make a believer out of anybody. We put on the most convincing pH dog and pony show ever staged.

We had also decided to make the show the occasion for our first annual rep sales meeting. We booked our rooms and the show booth space, got confirmations from all of our reps that they would attend, and things couldn't have looked much better. If this show went according to plan, if it was well attended by the guys we needed to talk to, we would be able to prove to a sizable number of instrumentation engineers and technicians that we could do everything claimed in our ads and our literature. As Babe Ruth said, "It ain't braggin' if you can do it."

We made arrangements ten days in advance to have our booth shipped to Chicago, and the trucking company out of Los Angeles picked it up on schedule. Things were going very smoothly. Too smoothly. Two days before the show was to open, I flew to Chicago to get situated. I visited the exhibition hall, expecting to see our booth sitting in its assigned spot awaiting the union electricians (whom I had yet to contact). No booth. I immediately got on the phone with the trucking company, which had a huge depot in Chicago. It had no record of the shipment.

They immediately contacted Los Angeles. The booth was still there. In spite of being a bit angry and embarrassed in front of our reps, I have to give the trucking company an A+ for the way it handled the situation from that point on. It air-freighted the booth to Chicago, and we missed only one show day out of the four. We made sure everybody who walked by our space on that first day saw big signs that asked them to be patient: "UNI-LOC is Always Worth Waiting For."

And we were. We had a good show. Lots of potential users left our booth shaking their heads in disbelief. We sold a few instruments on the spot, and generated sufficient follow-up leads to ensure that more sales would be coming within a few weeks. I scheduled each rep to booth duty with me. They learned a lot more about our instruments and made some excellent contacts. Moreover, we had a profitable sales meeting with positive plans for penetrating the huge industrial pH market.

Another unexpected thing happened at the show. A corporate representative of Ronald Trist Controls, Ltd. of Great Britain made several trips to our booth and decided his company should represent UNI-LOC in Britain, Germany, and France. He was quite convincing and it was mighty tempting to open another market, but we declined because we simply weren't ready to support a new front. I told him that within two years we would be ready and we would contact them. And we did. We established Trist as our European rep two years later.

This being our first trade show I was naturally curious to see how much the show had cost us versus probable return. To pay for the show and all that went with it we needed to sell six extra instruments. We sold six instruments at the show. Moreover, we generated at least fifty solid leads, and orders materialized within four weeks. That is how I judged every future trade show. If I had thought we could break even with extra sales at the show, plus engage in a lot of potential user contact, we exhibited.

Stonewalled

But we still weren't getting anywhere with the engineering-constructors, the people who design and build new process plants. We simply couldn't get to first base with any of them, and we wanted our pH analyzers to be specified for *new industrial construction*. This was big business. Some of those new plants would start-up using more than 100 pH analyzers. This was the complete opposite of our experience in cooling water control, working with the "commercial" mechanical consulting engineers. Looking back, it is easy to see why. In the commercial building and shopping center market the mechanical consulting engineers never had to deal with pH control—until we came along. We were the first to prove our worth to them so they leaned on us for guidance. Not so with the engineering-constructors. Those guys had been specifying the same old pH analyzers since the Dark Ages, and they weren't about to change.

On the home front Ted Barben and Jack Horner were trying to crack the California-based engineering-constructor market, and our reps were making the same efforts in their respective regions, but so far no progress. Orders from *existing* industrial facilities like Monsanto were still dribbling in, though at a gradually increasing rate thanks to our ads and trade shows. But if we could only get some of these engineering-constructor bonanzas we would be looking at between 100 to 150 pH instruments in a single order. One day Horner got word from a Los Angeles-area nationally renowned refinery that a sister facility, bigger and more modern, was to be built somewhere in California. He got the name of the engineering-constructor in charge of design and construction; it was a firm located in Texas.

This time instead of sending Barben or Horner, I decided to do the pick and shovel work myself. There had to be much more to this engineering-constructor blackballing, or logjam, than met the eye. If we only had this problem with one or two engineering-constructors I would pass it off to a little hanky-panky, but to be frozen out by all of them all across the country indicated that something far more serious was going on. I had to identify the problem so we could plan our way around it. Once again I took a red-eye special, my intention being to camp on the engineering firm's doorstep until I got to see its chief instrumentation engineer. After that I would make some marketing calls. I slept on the plane, freshened up at the hotel and called for an appointment. To my surprise, I was given one for that afternoon.

The chief instrumentation engineer was a middle-aged man who had obviously been with the firm for many years. He was polite and personable, and after a few pleasantries allowed me to give him a complete sales pitch on UNI-LOC's pH analyzers. I pulled out all the stops this time and dropped the names of the many companies who were enthusiastic UNI-LOC users (several having had their original pH analyzers specified by this same engineer with whom I was now talking). He was very attentive and I completed my presentation without interruption.

After I had finished, he admitted to being aware of UNI-LOC and said that he had heard good things about our analyzers. He had little doubt that we could probably substantiate our claims of troublefree performance. But then came the bomb. "Mr. Thomas," he said, "be realistic. Come back after you've been in business twenty years and we'll specify your pH instruments on new plants." I was in a state somewhere between shock and disbelief. Of all the responses I expected that wasn't one of them. I wondered how anybody in the position this man was in could make such a statement. If he was typical of his peers in the many engineering-constructor firms across the nation we were in deeper trouble than I had ever imagined. Our old-line competitors must have been laughing themselves silly at our attempts to break in. I couldn't help wondering if someday we might be so firmly entrenched that we would be protected by these guys in the same way.

When I regained control of my initial rush of anger, I asked, "If we have to wait twenty years to get business from you engineering-constructors how are we to survive in the interim?" He replied, "Put yourself in my place, Mr. Thomas. I've been specifying pH analyzers manufactured by the two industry leaders for over twenty years, and I can't be faulted by anyone because those instruments are now the standards of the process industries." He continued, "If those instruments have inherent limitations our process customers have learned to live with those limitations, so we don't see any reason to stick our necks out." I retorted, "I would think you'd want to specify the best of everything for your clients, especially if the best is cost effective. Isn't that what engineering is all about?" He said, "That's not my job. My job is to specify what I know works because that's where our *legal* responsibilities lie, and if our clients want something different then they must accept full responsibility, *and direct us accordingly.*"

I couldn't think of anything to say that had a prayer of changing his mind, so I took my cue and prepared to leave. As we shook hands I said, "I must admit to being somewhat angry, but I want to thank you for your time and for being so candid. You don't know it, but you've given me the answer to our dilemma." He said, "How's that?" I answered, "You'll have to wait and see." On that note I left and decided against making any cold marketing calls on that trip. I wasn't in the mood. And I had work to do at home if we were to have a ghost of a chance of getting that order for 100 plus pH instruments. I wasn't giving up.

It was now after seven o'clock in Orange County. I called Horner before getting on the plane and told him, "I want you to pack two Model 1000s under your arm tomorrow morning and take them to the refinery, and give both of them to the instrumentation engineer. Ask him to install them on the dirtiest streams and the toughest applications he has, and after he's done evaluating them, however long it takes, either give us a check or we'll take them back, no charge." Jack said, "Things didn't go too well, huh?" I said, "Worse than that. Not worth a tinker's dam but as usual, we learned something. Our only chance to break this logjam is to squeeze these engineering-constructors between their clients and us. We've got to convince their clients, the plant owners and operators, to demand that their engineering-constructors specify UNI-LOC. The back door is the only one that's open."

Arriving home, I called a rare meeting of the five owner–managers and explained what we were up against with the engineering-constructors. We hashed it out for about an hour and kept coming back to the sad fact that the only course of action open to us for new industrial construction would be to make sure that hundreds of the *existing* major process plants in the country had a chance to evaluate our 1000s on a free trial basis. Because existing plant operators have contact with prospective "new" plant operators, and because prospective new plant operators would be transferred from existing plants that had used UNI-LOC, sooner or later UNI-LOC would be demanded by all plant operators for new construction. It could be a long row to hoe, but it was the only row we had.

The plan we were hatching would represent by far the largest monetary investment we had ever made for inventory, which is why we needed a top-level meeting. Our plan was to have sufficient instruments on the shelf to support a large number of simultaneous evaluations, which would be staggered. It was hoped we would receive some payments along the way. We would allow sixty days for a free trial evaluation, and most likely could expect around 100 to 150 instruments in the field being evaluated at any given time. In other words, 100 to 150 instruments over and above normal production should see us through, although we would add more if needed.

Horner said the local refinery was surprised and pleased to get our Model 1000s for free trial; he would stay on top of it since time was of the essence, and would expedite those evaluations. I figured we had about ninety days before the new refinery pH analyzer specifications and requests for bid would be hitting the street.

This was obviously going to cost some money, but UNI-LOC was financially healthy. Our employment was in excess of

75 people and our growth was steady, if slow. We had added a couple of new reps in less important parts of the country. Water treatment systems sales were growing with the chemical companies playing a more active role. Our rep-dealer arrangement was working well with an occasional minor tiff over commissions. Were it not for the pesky obstacle of engineering-constructors freezing us out of new industrial construction, life would have been quite peaceful.

We were also getting lots of interest from venture capitalists who wanted in on our action. Even bankers were finding their ways to our door, and we had two large corporations, one on the New York Stock Exchange and another on the West Coast over-the-counter market, making acquisition noises. But we weren't tempted and gave them little of our time. The economy was recessive, and, as far as the stock market was concerned, bearish. We tried to listen politely to these overtures and give out very little information. Even Dun and Bradstreet couldn't do a real number on us except for our short-term credit rating as verified by our suppliers. We had no outstanding debt of more than thirty days. And we owner–managers now had salaries in the middle industry range for what we were supposed to be doing. We still didn't get extra pay for wearing more than one hat.

Full Steam Ahead

I called Cochrane Chase and told him to shag over to our office and be prepared to launch a new advertising campaign. He came that afternoon and we inaugurated our pH "Free Trial Program." We worked long and hard to discover just what needed to be said and how to say it in the fewest words. We were thinking of a full page ad in the *ISA Journal,* with smaller ads in *Petroleum Engineering* and *Chemical Engineering.* After we chewed everything over, Chase elected to pack up and get back on his own turf where he could think and pick his colleagues' brains. A couple of days later he walked in with a big skunk-eating grin on his face and said he was ready. That was fast work. I was anxious to see what he had—and I got a *very* pleasant surprise. The ad proof showed a UNI-LOC Model 1000 faded in the background with a huge "pHREE!" in big letters across the top. Lower down, in smaller but bold print, the free trial program was explained succinctly, straight to the point. In essence, the ad said we would send interested parties a Model 1000 at no charge for sixty days and they could shake it down in any way they chose. If it didn't outperform any other pH analyzer they had ever seen, owned, or used, send it back. On the other hand, if they liked it, send a check.

That ad had reverberations like Hiroshima. Word on the street was that some of our big, old-line competitors' salesmen were drowning their sorrows in a local bar. Talk about being trapped. The only way to counter our new offensive and answer our challenge would be to offer the same thing, and there was no way they could do that. We would kill them head-to-head. We were going to break into this clique or, like a WWI French aviator, go down in flames.

The ad was a great success. We shipped what seemed to be an endless supply of Model 1000s and began our staggered sixty-day sweat-out cycle. We weren't concerned about passing honest evaluations, but we were concerned with the possibility that some of the "pHREE" trial requests may have come from curiosity seekers, and perhaps a few instigated by our competitors. It was a calculated risk. But what were our choices? We couldn't afford to wait twenty years to be accepted by the engineering-constructor fraternity. By that time our patent would have expired anyway, and we would have nothing unique to offer. (About this time our pH patent issued and we were granted all of our claims. Our corrosion interlock patent had already issued some months before and there again we got most of our claims. Two bell-ringers. Although we didn't know it then, we would soon be forced to validate our pH patent in court in the nastiest and most drawn-out litigation imaginable.) To the best of our ability, we did check out the companies that requested participation in our pHREE trial program, and, from what we could tell after talking with them on the phone, all were bona fide pH users.

Over the next sixty days good things were happening. None of our free trial Model 1000s were returned, and we actually received some checks. But the frosting on the cake would be the refinery where we were being evaluated under the worst possible conditions. We were hoping for a recommendation from the operating engineers of the new refinery to override their engineering-constructor and *specify UNI-LOC*. Horner had been staying in close touch with that one, and every day he relayed good reports to us on the tests. Finally, after about six weeks, the refinery engineers purchased the two evaluation units and ordered several more. Additionally, they told us they were strongly recommending our Model 1000s for installation throughout the new refinery. But the final decision wasn't theirs to make. We still had a few weeks to sweat.

In the meantime, we were receiving payment checks at an accelerated rate. We continued the pHREE ad for two more months. Between those ads and a few more trade shows, we figured we might be over the hump and could discontinue the free trial program. I know this sounds impossible but with all the free trials we sent out during those three consecutive months of advertising, which added up to over five months of evaluations, we never had a single Model 1000 returned as unsatisfactory. It was a great program, and our reps took full advantage of it to put pressure on the engineering-constructors in their regions.

About four weeks after the conclusion of the successful refinery evaluations we got the best news yet. The instrument specifications for the new refinery had come out for bid and were written around UNI-LOC. The ice was broken, and it hadn't taken twenty years. Did I call the engineering-constructor's chief instrumentation engineer and gloat? No. Never. After all, he was the one who had unknowingly shown us the way. We also found that, sure enough, the refinery owner and operators had taken full responsibility for the pH analyzer decision. What a wonderful vote of confidence. We were on cloud nine.

CHAPTER TWELVE
SELL OR GO PUBLIC?

Another unanimous management decision we made early in the game was to maximize profits with the idea of someday taking UNI-LOC public. My dad, a prominent Orange County stockbroker and office manager for one of the Big 5, convinced us that we couldn't have it both ways. That is, we couldn't pay ourselves big salaries and bonuses and expect to maximize our gain when it came time to either go public or sell. So we opted to keep our salaries on the lower side of high-tech electronics industry averages and our bonuses as well.

Going public in those days wasn't as easy as it is today. The very idea of bringing untried companies with no track records onto the stock market, like today's—actually yesterday's—dot-coms, was unheard of. In the 1960s and early 1970s no self-respecting brokerage firm would think of such a thing. Imagine having the gall to sell shares in a merchandising company that has absolutely nothing unique to offer. No patents. No copyrights. No exclusive merchandise. Nothing that anyone else couldn't do with a pot of easy money. And for the past ten years, the stock market has been overflowing with easy money. What a crapshoot!

When we began making plans to go public the requirements were most stringent. My dad was guiding us, and when we UNI-LOC owners agreed the time was right, that we had the track record to demand a higher than average share price for a new offering, we would take the plunge. We figured we still had between two to three years to go. In the meantime, we focused on the next phase of our business, which now included an R&D department under Phil Cardeiro, and some added management innovations to further enhance employee morale. Morale had always been high: We just wanted to keep it that way.

Until this point, Cardeiro was our only electronics engineer; we also had one draftsman and a couple of technicians. Of course, Ted Barben sometimes assisted in circuit design since his electronics skills had been well-honed over the past four years. But the "fun" was about to begin with the hiring of our first engineer from outside the company. I had been dreading this moment from day one. I can hire sales staff without much concern because it is easy for me to spot the strengths and the human frailties of sales people. To a large extent they are stereotyped. And manufacturing types are relatively easy to screen, too, as are office workers and technicians.

But how do you find engineers of Cardeiro's caliber? You don't on the open market unless you are lucky enough to get a kid fresh out of school who turns out to be intuitively bright and creative. Engineers like Cardeiro and Barben either have their own companies or they are well up the ladder in some large bureaucracy and have no stomach for entrepreneurial adventures. I worked with enough engineers at North American and Northrop to know that fewer than five percent were truly creative. The remainder solved technical problems through the routine processes of elimination as taught in school. What worried me was that we had been spoiled for four years by having two of the best. Since engineering can easily become the biggest financial burden for a company like ours, not to mention the discipline that can screw-up monumentally, I was very concerned. How do we hire outsiders expecting them to be creative and inventive between the hours of eight and five, and who would devote all of their creative energies to our endeavor? I could envision hiring a battalion of engineers when we were trying to find just one who was truly innovative.

We now had more than 100 employees and were beginning to stretch our 16,000-square-foot plant to capacity. With the pressure temporarily off sales, every Monday morning I began the day by wandering around the factory and sitting down alongside some of our assemblers, picking up a tool, and joining them in the assembly of a circuit board or whatever, all the time visiting with them about anything and everything except business. Most assemblers were women, and they seemed to enjoy our visits together. (By the way, UNI-LOC was always an equal pay for equal work employer. Our salary increments applied to everyone.) I got to know all of our factory employees quite well. I don't know if they learned much from me, but I learned a lot from them. I relished those Monday mornings as much as anything I did at UNI-LOC. They were a lot more productive and satisfying than attending service club or civic meetings. Those exercises are better suited for presidents and CEOs who feel the need to network.

Because of those Monday morning visits I saw the need for a "Communications Committee." Our employees wanted some way to communicate their minor grievances to management—and vice versa. So we set up a mechanism. They elected three representatives from the factory, and together with three of us from top management, we gathered once per week in the conference room for one hour (on company time). We made it clear that the exchanges made in the committee meeting would be a two-way street. They would tell us what they would like to see in the way of improvements and we would do likewise. Although there were some doubts on the part of my colleagues, over time the committee proved successful. It was another way to solidify our company–employee relationships during those hectic growth periods.

Industry Recognition

Business rolled right along with few real problems, certainly nothing compared to what we had already been through. Orders were steadily growing; they were now coming from all segments of our markets, even the engineering-constructors. Proof of this came when one of our two old-line competitors, Foxboro, requested a license to design and manufacture pH analyzers under the UNI-LOC patent. In a way this was a surprise and in another way it wasn't. Foxboro is a first-class established manufacturer of many different types of instrumentation. Our pH analyzers interfaced with their proportional controllers in many industrial applications more often than not. We were flattered to be officially recognized by an industry leader. Such recognition, we felt, would once and for all dispel any lingering doubts about UNI-LOC held by a handful of stubborn engineering-constructors. The entire industry would know that one of the oldest, most respected leaders in pH control was now under license from UNI-LOC.

Did we really want early competition? No. But no matter how strong we thought our patent was, we had to keep in mind that in a highly technological society like ours, someone will eventually find another way to skin the cat. We knew that sooner or later we would get some competition, and we would rather it be from a large, well-respected company that acknowledges our position in the marketplace than from some schlocky operator who had nothing to lose by infringing our patent. (Alas, history would prove me wrong on that score. We eventually got an infringer all right, but one who was loaded with assets and had no fear of us or the courts.)

Furthermore, the electronics industry was on the threshold of the microcircuits and chips era. Almost anything was becoming possible with new exotic components hitting the market so fast we could barely keep up with them. We knew it was only a matter of time before another way to pre-amplify glass electrodes might be uncovered. We agreed to the patent license, and within a couple of months we got some competition from our new licensee, Foxboro.

But there was plenty of business out there for both of us. The market was growing by leaps and bounds. Not only did we have tons of old industrial pH equipment to retrofit, new applications were popping up every day where "on-line" pH measurement and control had never before been possible—traditional batch processes prevailing. In batch processing, a quantity of product is made in a huge kettle that is constantly stirred by paddles, and every few minutes a small sample is taken to the laboratory for a pH test. Then someone opens a valve feeding acid or alkali into the kettle to readjust the pH, and when it is finally correct, the batch is released for bottling, canning, or whatever the next step is. But batch processing became partially obsolete, thanks to UNI-LOC. Liquids and slurries could now more often be *continuously flow-processed*—no kettles necessary—with valves being proportionally opened and closed by commands from our pH analyzers as the liquid flowed through the pipes. Where on-line processing is used the savings are enormous!

Several months earlier, we had the good fortune to add to our ranks one D. Wesley Coombe. Coombe had been one of my seven "Executive Council" bosses at NLS—a V.P.—and was also its comptroller, the best one we could have hoped for. He was also my good old golfing buddy, many years earlier having been city champion of Toronto prior to emigrating to the U.S. Anyway, Wes had regularly kept in touch with me during the previous three years, and when he decided to leave NLS, he called and asked, "Have you got room for a broken-down accountant who doesn't need much money but wants something exciting to do?" I answered, "Hell, yes. The pay is low, the work endless, benefits scarce, but excitement we've got." He said, "You've got a deal, and we'll work out the details whenever we get around to it." A couple of weeks later he came up to Irvine and started out part-time, gradually becoming full-time as we grew.

Normally, I would never have made a unilateral decision like hiring Wes Coombe on the spot without a top-level meeting with the other owner–managers. But in this case, I had absolutely no doubts about how Coombe would be accepted by my partners. Coincidentally, Eldon Means had been making noises that he would like to bail out of UNI-LOC and go prospecting for gold. Apparently he'd had that passion for a long time but hadn't said anything about it. One thing for sure, Eldon welcomed Wes Coombe with open arms because he was busy enough without the accounting chores, which he liked the least. Coombe, being a father figure, proved a stabilizing factor in our support operations. He just had a way about him that made people want to please him, and he was genuinely interested in his colleagues' lives. He had five grown, well-educated kids of his own and looked like the prototype good ol' dad, which he was, except on the golf course. He was exactly ten years my senior and at least that many years smarter. Boomer— his nickname thanks to his awesome drives—had been with us for about two years when the following incident took place. And yes, Eldon was still on board, too.

What Have We Done?

One day I received a telephone call from a vice president of Betz Laboratories, our number one water treatment chemical customer. He wanted to visit us the following week, and he planned to bring another vice president and their corporate secretary—a legal beagle—with him. That sounded pretty ominous, and when I asked what the visit was about he told me he would rather not go into it over the phone. I checked the following week's schedules with our boys and called Betz back to set a time. I asked if there was anything special we should prepare for the meeting and the answer was no, other than having our secretary reserve three rooms at a good hotel. I retorted, "Secretary? What's that? We don't have any around here. But don't worry, we'll get the rooms." In truth, we had one secretary for the entire company. She could take dictation and was a good typist, but I typed my own correspondence as I composed it. (And there were no word processors with spell-check in those days). This is another example of entrepreneurial triumph over impecuniousness.

Naturally, we owner–managers engaged in a few in-depth, soul-searching powwows between that phone call and their arrival. We knew things had been going too smoothly. Hell, we hadn't had a crisis for almost a month! But we couldn't begin to imagine what the problem might be. The thought of Betz perhaps wanting to acquire us did cross our minds but we couldn't understand why a chemical company would want to own an instrument company, although we had seen worse marriages on the parts of several sophisticated conglomerates.

When the men from Betz arrived, on schedule, we did everything we could to make them feel comfortable. We gave them the customary facility tour reserved only for our best customers, with Cardeiro, Barben, Coombe, and myself taking turns as guides. They were a congenial group and managed to put us at ease so far as our thinking something might be wrong was concerned. Following the tour and coffee, we retired to the conference room where they opened the gate with, "We want to acquire

UNI-LOC." Had this been anybody but Betz, a firm we knew and that was our best water treatment customer, we would have ended the meeting posthaste. We simply weren't for sale. But they went on to point out that a Betz–UNI-LOC marriage made great marketing sense. They outlined some of their chemical plans and how they were leaders in the development of polymers, which would revolutionize water treatment, and how our pH control devices were critical to polymer applications. They reassured us that they now realized that chemicals, no matter what kind, were all subject to instrumentation control if the intended results are to be achieved.

We told them it was our plan to take UNI-LOC public within the next three years, which we had to do to maximize our financial return for all we had gone through. They countered with some facts we didn't know. Betz had recently gone public on the East Coast over-the-counter market and its stock was just beginning to catch on, even in the lingering bear market that had prevailed for the past few years. Betz had been a family-owned business for more than eighty years and it didn't go public because it needed money. It was already loaded with cash. The problem was almost identical to that of the Oster brothers. Mr. Betz, Sr. was well up in age and wasn't in the best of health. But, unlike the Oster brothers who sold to Sunbeam, the Betz family elected to go public. Now they needed to do something worthwhile with all that extra money. They also made it clear that Betz stock still had a long way to climb to reflect the company's earnings and assets, and UNI-LOC could realize its dreams of going public by piggybacking on Betz stock. They had never made any acquisitions before and they wanted us to be their first. Flattering to say the least. We told them we would give their kind offer serious thought, and if we wanted to pursue the matter further we would get together again and discuss the details. In any event, we wouldn't leave them dangling. They understood that we UNI-LOC owners had a lot to think and talk about. That evening we all got better acquainted.

It so happened that three other companies were making acquisition noises, two were on the New York Stock Exchange and one other, which I mentioned before, was on the West Coast over-the-counter market. The interesting thing about the West Coast company was that it was a huge engineering-constructor, and one with whom we had enjoyed a fine relationship. That company had made no prior acquisitions either, and it too liked us very much. Actually, we liked them better than the New York big board companies, but their stock had been stagnant for years. It was bull–bear marketproof, a sign of stable management— but no good for stock appreciation. The big board companies both had created several divisions through acquisitions. Buying companies like ours was old hat to them and we didn't like that much either. Also, their stock reflected the Dow Jones averages, which were steadily drifting downward.

We decided to study Betz stock and see what the analysts had to say since it was brand new. My dad dug out everything his experts could find about Betz and turned the data over to Phil Cardeiro, our best bird dog when it came to the stock market. All the data on Betz was bullish. We knew what UNI-LOC was worth in dollars at that point, and we would never have settled for a penny less. But we had no idea if Betz would meet that number, although they would be buying us with cheap dollars when you take into consideration their current stock price versus the original issue price as paid to them by the underwriter.

I also did some independent sleuthing with a couple of other entrepreneurial enterprises that had recently been acquired. A very close acquaintance and neighbor had begun a specialty chemical company, smaller than UNI-LOC, which was acquired by PPG. He had opted for a stock-for-assets transaction, which was tax-free, but there was a two-year Securities and Exchange Commission (SEC) restriction on the sale of any of his shares. He did very well in the PPG stock—on paper.

Cardeiro wanted us to hold off and go public. Jack Horner and Eldon Means wanted to sell to Betz, if the price was right. Both wanted a little of the good life and, of course, Eldon wanted out so he could go prospecting. Ted Barben also leaned toward selling, although he wasn't vocal about it. I was neutral at that point. After many discussions, it was decided that we would invite Betz back and talk about the terms of our possible acquisition.

To tell the truth, curiosity was killing us. The same three Betz execs arrived the following week, two came with golf clubs. Coombe and I teamed up, and we didn't play "customer" golf either. We beat them, but not badly. It was a congenial foursome and laid the groundwork for openness during our forthcoming negotiations. Betz had two numbers in mind for the purchase of UNI-LOC, one if it had to pay cash and another if we would take stock, that being the customary way it is done. If we took Betz stock with prices where they were, their number was almost what we had in mind. We weren't far apart, but their offer would have to be sweetened. There were three of them negotiating against the five of us, with Cardeiro and me carrying the ball most of the time. I loved having Cardeiro in this kind of action because he was tougher than hell with money. I won't say he still had his first dollar, but he knew who did.

Our major objection was that we would be accepting Betz stock that would be SEC-restricted for two years before we could sell any. We wanted a stock-for-assets transaction all right because we didn't want to be taxed as we would if we took cash. True, sooner or later the piper has to be paid. We would be taxed when we finally could sell Betz stock at capital gains rates but by then we might have offsetting losses or depreciation from other investments. Anyway, our argument was that too much could happen in two years, so we would be risking the possibility of selling UNI-LOC at far too cheap a price by the time the money actually got to us. We argued back and forth for a few more hours and decided to continue the following day. At least twice during the negotiations the Betz boys left the room and called Jack Betz, the president and CEO who was the son of the founder, and asked how much running room they had with the price. Tomorrow we would find out.

That evening over dinner, we owner–managers got together for another session. Interestingly, our thoughts seemed to have changed regarding going public with UNI-LOC stock. Nobody was talking about it, not even Cardeiro, though I suspected he still would have preferred that to selling to Betz. Our thinking, though, was definitely in the direction of trying to find some way the Betz thing could work. It was a challenge. Now that I had more time to think about it, I leveled with my guys and told them how my dad had prepared me for what it would be like to be the CEO of a publicly traded company. He told me my life wouldn't be my own because stock analysts would be calling all the time wanting some inside dope on the company. Once a company is on the market the fiduciary responsibility to the shareholders is awesome, not to mention the concerns for one's own share prices.

This is one reason publicly traded companies become bureaucracies, if they aren't already. The reports and paperwork alone can drive an entrepreneur crazy. True, we might be able to talk Ward Carlson into taking the role of CEO for the benefit of stock analysts and shareholders, but Ward now had his own Amway business, which was growing by leaps and bounds. There was no guarantee he would be available. And I would never trust anyone else to come into our company at that level. I knew Cardeiro would have been comfortable and capable for a while in a bureaucratic CEO role, but his skills in engineering and manufacturing made him far too valuable to waste like that. For those reasons, I favored trying to make the Betz acquisition work. And for the first time, I understood and appreciated why the Oster brothers hadn't gone public.

Innovation Prevails

We got our heads together and concentrated on creating a mechanism that would reduce our risk should Betz stock be worth less in two years when we could legally sell it than it was now when we were making the deal. Suddenly the bell rang. To this day I'm not sure which one of us came up with the idea. It might have been Wes Coombe for all I remember. He was privy to all that was going on. The minute the words were uttered we all knew we had the answer. We were confident of a great three years ahead of us based on business already in progress plus near-term developments.

What we needed was a three-year earn-out period where a large number of extra Betz shares, over and above the initial buy-out shares, would be tied to UNI-LOC's performance. At the end of the earn-out period, if our profits before taxes were 100 percent higher than at the end of the year in which we made the deal, we would double our Betz shares. Anything in between would be prorated. This would be our final offer. It was a win–win deal. If we made our goal of a 100 percent profit increase, then Betz would have made an even sweeter deal no matter what its stock price was at the end of the earn-out. But if Betz stock decreased in value over the two-year SEC holding period, at least we would have partially protected our original selling value by having twice as many shares.

We met with the Betz troops at 10 a.m. the following morning and resumed haggling. After everyone had warmed up, we dropped our earn-out plan on the table and awaited their reaction. Dead silence! They asked to be excused, and retired to the other private room to talk amongst themselves. About a half hour later they returned, and we began discussing our plan in earnest. Once the details were thoroughly understood by both sides, they again withdrew to call Jack Betz. When they came back this time they had agreed to our plan in principle, but they wanted a two-year earn-out period with a possible 50 percent increase in Betz stock tied to a 50 percent increase in UNI-LOC's profits. We turned that down flat. Either we would get a 100 percent increase in stock for a 100 percent increase in UNI-LOC earnings over three years, plus our stipulated selling price, or we didn't have a deal. I reminded them that we would do far better than that in three years by going public. Once again, they retired to the private room and called Jack Betz. Fifteen minutes later they returned and said, "We've got a deal."

In retrospect, and there's always twenty-twenty hindsight, we should have held out for a 200 percent increase in stock in exchange for a 200 percent increase in profits over a four-year earn-out period because that is what we ended up doing. Anyway, we made the deal and received our shares, and the SEC clock began ticking.

Having a father who was a stockbroker, I was no stranger to the market. I had always been a small player, but I didn't subscribe to that old party line about "buy and hold," and neither did my dad. All it takes is one bad recession within a thirty-year period and most of your market gains can be wiped out. My dad was a believer in market timing, which, in fact, most brokers aren't sharp enough to play, and he always invested his own money where he invested his clients'. So even though I wasn't a regular player, I always made money. But I had control. I could either hold or sell. The choice was mine.

However, the Betz experience with the two-year SEC holding requirement was a different ball game. It was one of the most frustrating experiences of my life. And I had five years of restrictions to look forward to before I could sell *all* of my Betz stock, assuming I would ever want to: three years to the end of the earn-out plus two additional years of SEC restriction on those new earn-out shares.

Oh, I of little faith. The restriction period was heaven-sent, although none of us knew it at the time. Betz stock was, of course, listed in *The Wall Street Journal* so I could track it every day, which

I did in the beginning. But I soon had to divorce myself from that habit because I couldn't do anything about it anyway. From that time on I concentrated *only* on our earn-out.

As soon as the Betz deal was consummated, just for the heck of it I contacted my old neighborhood acquaintance who had sold his company to PPG. Like we had, he had taken shares in exchange for his company. But his PPG shares had tracked the Dow Jones downward slide, reflecting the mild recession, and his stock had already lost 20 percent of its value. He was fit to be tied because he still had eighteen months to go on his SEC restriction. Betz stock, on the other hand, moved steadily against the Dow and was the newest darling on the East Coast over-the-counter market. Of course, Betz's year-end numbers when combined with UNI-LOC's were fabulous.

Because Eldon Means had other plans and had elected to take cash for his UNI-LOC shares instead of Betz stock, he wasn't included in the earn-out exercise. He did eventually head for South America and went prospecting for gold. Wes Coombe, now a vice president and member of our management team, took over Eldon's responsibilities.

There was one vitally important provision in the acquisition agreement between Betz and UNI-LOC without which our earn-out could have been compromised. *For the entire three-year earn-out period, we managers and previous owners of UNI-LOC had complete control of all that UNI-LOC did.* We answered to no one until that period was over. However, we did agree to have two *nonvoting* Betz members on our Board of Directors, and Betz chose the same two vice presidents who had negotiated our acquisition. We found the new Betz–UNI-LOC board members to be very, very helpful, contributing some excellent ideas. They offered their services in every way that might contribute to our well-being. They also offered us money if we needed it, which we didn't.

Thanks to them, we adopted the Betz medical plan for our employees since it was superior to ours; we also adopted the Betz employee retirement package. Furthermore, they couldn't help noticing that we were bulging at the seams in our present facility, so they talked us into allowing Betz to finance a new plant. We then initiated plans for our 53,000-square-foot facility, which was to be located a few blocks away.

CHAPTER THIRTEEN
EUROPE

In the new Betz–Uni-Loc era, we continued to get a lot of business from the Bell Telephone companies across the country. Our local field service department under Leo Hendrikx was now a prosperous profit center, servicing Pacific Telephone and several high-rise real estate complexes. The phone company had decided early in the game that the most cost-effective way to handle it was to have us check and service their UNI-LOC cooling water control systems monthly. Water treatment control was growing, and we had few problems other than that our good dealer friend Mogul feared that we would cut off its supply of custom UNI-LOC systems now that we were owned by Betz. I took a trip to Cleveland to put that fear to rest. UNI-LOC and its reps scrupulously avoided the chemical end of things with respect to the water treatment marketplace, and our reps were admonished to never recommend Betz over any other chemical supplier-dealer. We were 100 percent in the instrumentation and control systems business. Period.

We founded a small division that we called "Micro Sensors" and added it to our UNI-LOC–Betz family for the sole purpose of manufacturing pH glass electrodes. Electrode costs were among our larger outlays for parts. We had been using Swiss-made glass electrodes with excellent results, but prices were becoming unstable, thanks to the dollar devaluing against the Swiss franc. However, manufacturing wasn't an easy road either. Learning to blow glass didn't happen overnight. Like the wood plugs in our pH reference cells, glass electrodes were more an art than a science. We ran into all kinds of problems maintaining consistent glass formulas, and, for a while, we were getting rejections from the field because of higher-than-normal impedance. Glass electrodes always have high impedance, but ours went too far beyond specifications. But we persevered. After a few months we were producing excellent electrodes.

The earn-out was progressing smoothly, and our sales and profit objectives were being met either on or ahead of schedule. The time had come to take a look at opening up Europe as a future market. Initially we would exploit our Model 1000 pH analyzer rather than cooling water systems since the 1000s didn't require water treatment training and were much easier to install for demonstrations. During the next two years I took five trips abroad to launch UNI-LOC in the European industrial marketplace. We set up Ronald Trist Controls, Ltd. in the U.K. as our main representative. Trist also had offices in Germany and France, and we found a good potential rep contact in Holland, the Van Hengel Company. Trist was a willing group, and was a fairly large manufacturing company in its own right, specializing in boiler controls. But pH was new to them, and none of us had any idea of what we were in for. The European experience was just that, a frustrating experience for the first couple of years.

In the early 1970s most European nations had erected artificial barriers to foreign competition in high-tech markets. The most insidious of those barriers were the "ICI" safety tests in the U.K. and the "PTB" safety tests in Germany, which Holland and France accepted as well. Both the PTB and ICI tests were nitpicking, comprehensive product tests that made our Underwriters Laboratory (UL) requirements look like a stroll in the park (and made some of our more perverse engineering-constructors back home look rather open-minded). These tests were an undisguised barrier that would take at least eighteen months to pass, due to the many levels of government bureaucracy along the way. Their hope was that outsiders trying to pass those tests would soon become discouraged and go home. This was no place for entrepreneurs. Nevertheless, we plugged along and, thank goodness, our reps handled some of the leg work. All we did back home was keep making changes in our pH analyzers to satisfy their demands until there was nothing left to change.

Things are much different today, thanks to the Common Market and various international agreements on free—or at least semi-free—trade. But much of the credit goes to Margaret Thatcher, former Prime Minister of Britain. Europe and the U.K. were socialized in the 1970s and 1980s, and nobody but the Germans worked very hard. All had tariff barriers protecting their own favorite markets. The British were the worst. As I said, the British ICI tests and the German/French/Dutch PTB tests were typical additional barriers. Fortunately, the ICI and PTB tests applied *only to hazardous environment applications,* so we were able to make inroads into the paper, distilling, food, and water pollution abatement markets while awaiting ICI and PTB approvals. Tough sledding, though, slow going.

Additionally, the Europeans and the British knew next to nothing about sales as an independent business. There were no established sales representative companies like the ones in the States, so we had to do what everyone else from the U.S. did. We joined up with a company (in our case, Ronald Trist Controls) that manufactured their own products. They would sell our products along with theirs, when possible. This wasn't ideal, but it was all we had.

Thatcher's reforms included privatizing the many heavy industries owned and operated by the government. She lowered the marginal income tax rates from over 90 percent to 40 percent, allowing people to keep some of their money, and she lowered or eliminated many tariffs. This forced *both* British management and labor to get off their butts and go to work. Prior to that time it was common to see middle management coming in at 9 a.m., leaving at 1 p.m. for a three-hour pub lunch with a couple pints of ale, and dragging back to work for an hour before going home. It was known as the British disease.

Today nothing like that could be further from reality. The old guard is gone; there is a different generation with an achievement ethic. With the elimination of tariffs, plus privatization, there is no choice but to *compete* or perish.

As an example, I have a very close friend in the U.K., Philip Meeson, who is chairman and CEO of the Dart Group. It is a holding company that owns Channel Express freight airlines with a fleet of Airbusses and a variety of other aircraft operating internationally; Fowler-Welch national produce distributors; Ben-Air Freight Forwarding, which operates internationally, heavily in the Orient; and is now in the throes of starting a new, low-cost passenger airline, JET 2, with 737s operating from the Leeds-Bradford International Airport in the U.K. to Europe. I predict that this airline will become the British version of Southwest Airlines.

When I first met Philip he was 22 years old and fresh out of the RAF. (I met him through aviation activities, and we did a lot of flying together during my visits to the U.K.) He became Britain's national aerobatic champion; by saving money earned from his exhibition flying over the years, he finally was able to secure a loan from a bank to buy one old freight airplane. Working around the clock, like we entrepreneurs do, the rest is history. Philip comes from a working-class family, and came up through the transition period from the old Britain to the new; he is one of the new breed who made the transition possible. This success story would not have been possible thirty years ago.

Opening a European market nowadays is just a little more difficult than operating in the U.S. But be sure to work through a good import–export bank and have your *letters of credit* in order. You don't want to ship any products overseas, except to your own subsidiaries, without guarantee of payment in advance.

When in Europe . . .

On my first trip to Paris, I met with Monsieur Louis Marchant, the French regional manager for Trist. I was alone and quite apprehensive. Our German PTB tests were in progress but we were still some months from passing. While in Europe I wanted to show him a Model 1000 to see if he thought he could sell it. Of course, like every dumb American I expected Marchant to speak to me in English. After all, wasn't English the acknowledged international trading language? Yes, but somebody forgot to tell the French.

My mother was French, and in my very early days we spoke some French in our home, but that was so long ago and I didn't remember much. To speak to Mr. Marchant, I had to whip out my little tourist language book and muddle along. But when the clock struck 5 p.m., he shifted gears, and, still in French, invited me to the bistro for a libation. God, what a relief. I happily accepted. No sooner had the drinks arrived and we toasted our tentative future when he began speaking impeccable English. I was flabbergasted. I asked him, "Why in the world did you make me murder the French language for two hours when we could have communicated so beautifully in English?" "Monsieur Thomas," he answered, "when we are in France, *and we are doing business*, we speak French." You know, that's pretty clever.

On that same trip I was joined in Germany by another dear friend now in heaven, Richard Allen, managing director of Ronald Trist Controls. He wanted to personally introduce me and UNI-LOC to his German regional manager, Werner Timm, who had already set in motion the German PTB testing. During the war Timm had been a ranking German officer, and he looked the part. He was stately and somewhat formal, but very polite, quick and witty, and full of enthusiasm for the new Germany.

On the other hand, Richard Allen, Timm's boss, was a bushy eye-browed bulldog Winston Churchill-type, who had been a pathfinder in the RAF, a lead pilot flying Lancaster bombers who led many raids over Germany. Nonetheless, the two men obviously admired each other and got on very well. Both had well-honed senses of humor.

We were meeting in the beautiful city of Duesseldorf, and at dinner I happened to mention what a lovely and unusually modern city it was. Immediately, Werner began extolling its many virtues and how it was truly the most modern city in Germany. This went on for some time when Richard calmly took a sip of his Cognac and a puff off his cigar and said, "Werner, Duesseldorf should be a modern city. We blew the shit out of the old one!" Now, in this age of political correctness you may think things went downhill after that, but they didn't. I can tell you that before the evening ended Timm got even, and I had some of the heartiest laughs of my life.

Upon returning home I found they hadn't even missed me at UNI-LOC. I should have gone to the Riviera. The company was running like a well-oiled machine. Well, maybe they did miss one thing. I had a habit every morning, following the mail delivery, of yelling across the bullpen to Coombe, asking if we got any new orders. He would always yell back whatever we got or didn't get. It became a ritual and it bugged Cardeiro no end. He would get livid because he felt I was more concerned with new purchase orders than with shipments. I never asked about shipments or billings because I knew with the earn-out carrot dangling in front of our noses those were okay. But Cardeiro used to get so angry, and he would yell at me that shipments were more important than my damn orders because we couldn't be paid until after we shipped. And I would answer something like, "Hey, man, getting new orders is our life's blood. Shipping the stuff out the back door should be a piece of cake by now." Whatever we said was always ad lib and never failed to get a few laughs. We had a lot of fun and the needle was always out. Nobody escaped.

Over the next few months UNI-LOC was very busy and thankfully without any new crises. Our Betz stock was still climbing, the opposite direction of the market. Although we didn't talk about it much, we were still mighty concerned about fickle stock market investors. If some political leader misses a bowel movement the market burps, or sometimes for no reason at all companies lose favor with flaky investors who get off the train as fast as they got on. (They call it profit taking.) The way Betz stock was performing we couldn't help but wonder when the bubble would burst. But it didn't that first year of the earn-out. In fact, Betz split its stock, and it wasn't long before it slowly began climbing back to the level where it had split. Against the bear market, Betz and UNI-LOC were defying the law of gravity.

A Stroke of Good Luck

We had finally hired some engineers and our R&D group was researching possible additions to our pH analyzer product line. We were even doing a little basic research in the area of endo-thermic cells, a far-out way of producing cold instead of heat. This wasn't high priority, but we thought it deserved some investigation. I was far too busy handling both sales *and* marketing, so I began to explore ways to spin off sales to someone else. Jack Horner wasn't an inside man, so he would remain doing what he was doing, which didn't hurt his feelings one bit. And besides, there was no better troubleshooter in the field than Jack. Then another unexpected thing happened, a fall-out of the Betz–UNI-LOC marriage, that solved my dilemma about how to lighten my load. We inherited Betz's one and only instrument engineer, a man they had hired a few years before when we first began supplying them with custom instruments. Betz knew its chemical salesmen were going to need technical back-up with system applications and start-ups, so it hired a sharp young instrumentation engineer named Carl Frova to handle that. When we were acquired, Betz didn't know what to do with Frova, so they asked if we could use him. It was fairly obvious to me that Betz really wanted us to hire Frova. They liked him, felt responsible for him, and I think they wanted someone they had worked with, who knew instrumentation, to better assess what UNI-LOC was doing.

So on my first routine trip back to Trevose, Pennsylvania, where Betz had recently moved into new quarters, I interviewed Carl Frova. This took place about one month following the acquisition. I not only found him to be a capable instrument engineer with broad chemical engineering exposure, I felt he was also a natural born salesman who apparently didn't know it. He had never been exposed to actual sales, but he did have lots of customer contact through his support of Betz's chemical salesmen. Once again my bell rang, and I approached him on the possibility of joining UNI-LOC as our *eastern sales* ramrod, supporting our reps technically and also doing sales back-up, with the long-term goal of becoming our eastern sales manager. He would still live in Doylestown and continue working out of Betz office space. It wasn't easy to judge his reaction but I knew the wheels were turning. He knew he could get as good a job as the one he had with any number of instrument companies, but he would have to move and his wife loved Doylestown. So, he agreed to think about my proposition, talk it over with his wife, and get back to me. I finished my other Betz business and headed for home.

A few days later I got a call from Frova requesting a visit to UNI-LOC, he wanted to look our operation over and get acquainted with our key people. That sounded fine to me because I didn't want to make him a serious offer unless UNI-LOC management concurred. Frova spent the better part of a work week with us. At the end of his visit, he said he would take the job as UNI-LOC's eastern ramrod if it was open to him and if he didn't have to take a salary cut. My guys gave their blessings and Frova moved onto UNI-LOC's payroll. As I said earlier, I had a hunch Betz leaned on Frova to join us because they wanted some kind of a pipeline into our everyday operations. Fair enough. I would probably have done likewise.

I immediately arranged another trip east to introduce Frova to the eastern reps. (Everything east of the Mississippi was his to support.) The reps were enthusiastic about having technical support much closer to their territories.

I have to tell you about Frova's first UNI-LOC rep sales meeting, which took place during another ISA Show. By then, I had seen him in action a few times giving presentations to small groups. He was very impressive, a born salesman with a great sense of humor and timing. And being Italian, he is very animated, talking with his hands as much as with his mouth. That coupled with his dry humor could have qualified him as a stand-up comedian. Anyway, Frova was scheduled to deliver a presentation at our rep sales meeting, and this would be his first "performance." I had been teasing him about talking with his hands and he said, "I don't have to use my hands!" So, I bet him twenty-five dollars that he couldn't make the presentation with his hands in his pockets. His response was, "In a pig's eye!" So he walked to the podium, put his hands in his pockets, looked around the room smiling, and said, "Umm…er…uh…ahh…. Oh what the hell!" Out came his hands, he made a great presentation, and I collected twenty-five clams. Carl Frova turned out to be a worthy asset to UNI-LOC. We couldn't have done better if we had been out searching for someone like him.

The time had come for me to relinquish day-to-day control over sales since I would be spending more time on marketing and playing the role of president, which, with Betz in the picture, was now more demanding. And I would continue to open up Europe. For the first time, my days as an entrepreneur were showing signs of becoming numbered. We also put our plans for Ted Barben on hold in favor of redirecting his efforts toward the western sales manager's job. Everything west of the Mississippi would be his. He was as well qualified to manage our reps in the west as Frova was by now in the east. From that point forward my role in sales was to set policy and to support our sales managers with marketing activities. Barben accepted his new role with his customary enthusiasm and went on to do another great job. Horner took over Barben's consulting engineer accounts, combining them with his own. He continued to operate independently as our "roving" consulting engineer specialist and applications troubleshooter.

A Drop of the Loch

Over the next eighteen months I continued to work Europe, trying to jar that market off dead center. We had made a little positive progress in the U.K. Ronald Trist Controls added a hard-working young sales engineer who understood pH and all that went with it, and who had sold a few Model 1000s in Britain despite those ongoing ICI safety tests. His name was Ken MacAlpine, a well-educated young Scotsman from the north country.

He wanted me to accompany him on some sales calls, which I was delighted to do. He also suggested a distillery tour. Unbeknownst to me, our pH analyzers were being used in distilleries. Oh joy!

We headed first for Aberdeen where the world's oldest paper mill, the Wiggins-Teape mill, was still in operation—and it used UNI-LOC Model 1000s. Word had it that this was an unprofitable mill because of its age, but it produced the world's finest parchment. I could envision a potentially great story here for advertising purposes. We arrived at the mill only to find it closed, with armed guards everywhere—and the guards were obviously American. We cautiously ventured up to the main gate where we were politely informed that the mill was closed for ten days. That was that. Undaunted, Ken contacted one of the mill foremen at home and asked him to join us at the pub for a couple of pints. The foreman told us that the U.S. government takes over the Wiggins mill once every year, retaining the chief papermaker, but bringing its own operating staff and armed guards. They spend the next two weeks making the super-special paper used in United States currency. When done, they quietly fill a fleet of lorries (trucks) and proceed to the seaport, where paper, staff, guards, and all are loaded onto a ship back to the States. So much for my advertising coup.

We visited several other mills, made some cold sales calls, and decided to head for the distillery tour. This turned out to be a three-day affair during which we visited nine distilleries. Not only did we get a full tour of each one, but every master distiller took us into his office, sat us down, and poured us a few of his choicest offerings. We sampled every conceivable Scotch from single malts to blends, many of which are not available here. Some were twenty-five years old and not offered on any market. It was an aesthetic experience. We were also served lunches in the executive dining room, complete with wine, followed by Cognac and cheese. I think we were on our own in the evenings, but I don't remember eating dinner. I crashed into bed.

By the end of the three days, Ken and I were pretty well anesthetized, and that's when he came up with the idea of driving further north to show me his beloved Scotland at its best. He was getting sentimental. He then said we might even see a dreaded Haggis. I remember asking what a Haggis was, but all I could glean was something to the effect that it was the meanest, ugliest, most ferocious beast on the face of the earth, only found in the north country of Scotland.

I had been looking forward to a weekend of sleep, but MacAlpine would have none of that—and it was his car. Feeling no pain, we headed for the hills, and by happenstance ended up at Rob Roy's grave. We were standing on the grave slab when Ken, looking even more somber and with tears in his eyes, decided that since Rob Roy was such a famous patriot, and if it hadn't been for him we might not have had any distilleries to tour, we owed him a toast. So we climbed back into the car, put it on autopilot, found a purveyor of adult beverages and bought a bottle of Scotch, a small bottle of vermouth, a tiny bottle of orange bitters, crushed ice, a cocktail shaker, and some plastic glasses. We found our way back to the cemetery, took our booty to the grave, and in solemn formality mixed a few shakersfull of Rob Roy cocktails—sharing them with the other grief-stricken mourners. We all drank toasts to the hero until we depleted our supply of elixir, at which time we departed in search of a Haggis. Did we find one? No, thank God and it's just as well. It would have been a lose–lose encounter. The Haggis would have eaten us for dinner and then died of alcohol poisoning.

MacAlpine then took me to the airport and put me on a plane for New York. I slept the entire trip and somehow made the transfer to my flight to L.A. By the time I reached Orange County I was back among the living and vowed never again to consider another such adventure.

Things at UNI-LOC were normal with sales and production increasing steadily. Betz stock had continued its slow but steady rise and was now approaching that magic level where it had last split. It split again a few months before the end of our initial SEC restriction.

CHAPTER FOURTEEN
AN UNEXPECTED CHALLENGE

Shortly after my return from Scotland, the largest of our two competitors introduced its new pH analyzer, which featured a transmitter electrode. It used FETs to pre-amplify the electrode current just as ours did and, from the magazine ads, it looked like a probable infringement of our patent. We managed to get some of the company's literature and, sure enough, it was obvious even to the untrained eye that this device was a copy of the UNI-LOC analyzer. We contacted our patent attorney who did some research and concluded that we were right. He suggested we send the offending company a letter to put them on notice and to offer to license them under the same terms and conditions as we had with Foxboro (our other competitor who had already taken a license). We agreed, and the letter was sent.

Today the latest buzzwords for patent protection are "intellectual property rights." Law firms are coming out of the woodwork wanting to perform intellectual property audits for your company. Sounds good, but who knows if they are qualified? Back when UNI-LOC got its patents, and again when some UNI-LOC founders received additional patents for our successor companies, we always used patent attorneys for such matters. Take my advice and deal only with bona fide patent and trademark attorneys in intellectual property rights matters. Trade secret issues may be another matter, sometimes those involve restraint of trade or antitrust law, but a patent attorney can direct you to a specialist if you need one.

A few weeks passed and our patent attorney finally heard from our adversary's patent attorney, a venerable old law firm with lots of clout and a client list that reads like who's who. Their position was that no infringement existed because UNI-LOC did not have a valid patent. That, by the way, is a predictable response. They were assuming either we didn't have the money to defend our position or that we would be afraid to take a chance, because if we lost the case that would invalidate our patent. But they forgot that if we didn't litigate we would lose our patent anyway. They had underestimated us, as big companies often do with small companies.

We were angry that the undisputed leader in pH control dismissed UNI-LOC's contribution to the art, completely ignoring what our analyzers had done for liquid process control, cooling water control, and pollution abatement. They should have accepted the fact that just because they had been the pioneers in pH measurement they did not automatically own the rights in perpetuity to all that follows. This was ego, and it turned out to be one of the costliest ego trips any landmark company ever took.

There was, however, one nagging thought in my mind, and I don't remember ever discussing it with my partners. If UNI-

LOC defended its patent through litigation and lost, thus invalidating our patent, would we then owe Betz, now our parent company, reparations since the UNI-LOC they had purchased would no longer have the exclusivity in the marketplace that it did at the time of the acquisition? A sticky question.

This situation dragged on for a couple of years, with nasty letters flowing back and forth. It was sometime after I had retired from UNI-LOC that the decision was made to file suit against the alleged infringer. Nobody seemed to be in any rush to talk, and the defendant, meanwhile, continued business as usual, manufacturing and selling lots of its copycat pH analyzers—even after being put on notice and being sued. That was the risky part, and the height of conceit. Looking back, I believe they took the calculated gamble that the court would be impressed by their having no fear of the validity of UNI-LOC's patent and manufactured their analyzers with impunity.

The case took about four years to come to trial, with no indication of a possible out-of-court settlement. In the interim, depositions were taken on both sides, and the costs must have been astronomical for the defendant. Because our parent company had its own in-house patent counsel, UNI-LOC's costs were much less. The trial was quite a circus with the defendant grandiosely trying to prove that UNI-LOC's transmitter electrodes were nothing that wasn't obvious to anyone skilled in the art. In other words, every pH manufacturer would have eventually done what UNI-LOC had done had they been the first to discover field effect transistors (FETs). Hell, you could say that about most inventions. Somebody discovers something new and combines it with something old and creates a unique gizmo—and does it first. That is what patents are supposedly all about.

Each of our twenty-odd patent claims were systematically attacked and dismembered. Most were thrown out as invalid. Again, that is standard procedure. Nobody ever gets all claims validated. The defendant contended it had been experimenting for years with vacuum tube electrometers to pre-amplify the pH glass electrode current, proof to them that the idea wasn't new—which it wasn't. But UNI-LOC was still the first to find a way to do it, which didn't seem to impress the judge. The original ideas for getting to the moon weren't NASA's either, but NASA was the first to get there.

Anyway, one of the unique features of Phil Cardeiro's—UNI-LOC's—invention, which was almost an afterthought, had to do with the impedance of the pre-amplifier being matched to the impedance of the glass electrode throughout a wide range of temperature changes of the fluid being measured, that is, when FETs were used as Cardeiro had used them. The defendant had no rebuttal for that one.

The judge found in favor of UNI-LOC, and leveled treble damages against the defendant, which amounted to a king's ransom. The treble damages resulted from the fact that the defendant had continued manufacturing and selling its infringing devices *after* UNI-LOC had put it on notice. This judgment took place about four years after I retired, so I wasn't privy to the details, but as I understand it the final settlement was satisfied not with cash. The defendant gave UNI-LOC its entire *industrial pH division as payment*. Scratch one big competitor. Had the defendant ceased manufacturing and selling infringing analyzers between our notice and the trial, it still would have lost the case, but no huge damages would have been assessed. It then could have remained in business, taken a license from UNI-LOC, and continued as a leader in industrial pH control. Again, there are great lessons to be learned from this one.

Shifting Frova and "The Weapon"

We had now completed the second year of our earn-out period, and the original issue of Betz stock was unrestricted and could be sold. All of us did sell some, and suddenly the trappings of affluence began to appear. The price was up. So far, we had quadrupled the stock's worth. Lovely. Now we were into the last year of the earn-out and looking forward to doubling our shares, which at this time looked like a lead-pipe cinch. My neighbor who had sold his company to PPG more than two years before had a different experience. His stock had lost fifty percent of its value before it became unrestricted. The sad part was that he did have to sell most of his stock—to clear his debts. A big spender, he had gone out on a limb, thinking he would be in fat city by the time his stock became unrestricted. He didn't have an earn-out program either. Nothing to offset his loss in stock value. But he still had his CEO's job, though, and from the looks of things he would need it for a long time.

UNI-LOC sales were growing rapidly, and we needed a full-time manufacturing manager. Cardeiro had worn two hats, engineering and manufacturing, long enough. It was time for Carl Frova to move to Orange County from Pennsylvania and take over UNI-LOC sales, allowing Ted Barben to become our vice president in charge of R&D and manufacturing. At first, Frova had a hard time adjusting to the idea of moving west. He and his wife were hard-core easterners. But we prevailed because there was simply no other choice. We could no longer justify having two regional sales managers when either Frova or Barben were now qualified to handle it all. And we were definitely not going outside for a manufacturing manager when we had our own entrepreneurial talent to exploit. So Carl and his family moved to Newport Beach and rapidly became acclimated to the Southern California lifestyle.

Barben took over manufacturing and R&D with relish. One of the first things he did was install a computer-controlled inventory system. He wasn't the last of the big spenders, but he was working on it. (Jack Horner could put everybody to shame when it came to spending money, but fortunately for UNI-LOC he didn't have a departmental budget. He operated from mine, and getting money out of me was like asking the Pope for a donation.) Computer programs in those days were in their infancy—an understatement—but in true Barben fashion, he hung in there, refusing to admit defeat. To this day, I'm not sure if our computer inventory program was cost effective, but, by golly, we were one of the first to have one, for whatever that's worth.

Back to Europe

Before the end of the earn-out period, I still had one more European sales trip to make, this time to the Netherlands. We had a dynamite Dutch rep by the name of Cor Van Hengel, who had done well for us almost everywhere in his territory, which included Holland and Belgium. But for some reason he had hit a brick wall at Royal Dutch Shell in Rotterdam, and he wanted me to help him out. He was pursuing an order for a large quantity of analyzers for a new facility Shell was building in Borneo.

This had all the earmarks of another engineering–constructor saga, and, as it turned out, it was. The chief instrumentation engineer at Shell made that fellow in Texas, the one who had told me to come back in twenty years, look like the most flexible man you would ever want to deal with. Now, most Dutch people I know are affable, friendly, and very nice. (I'm married to one from the old country and she's great!) But I can't think of a sufficient number of derogatory adjectives to describe this particular chief engineer. He was one of the most egotistical, pompous, boisterous, bombastic bastards I had ever met. The champion! He wasn't the least bit interested in anything we had to say. He couldn't stop bragging long enough.

He had a favorite pH manufacturer, and it wasn't UNI-LOC—despite the fact that Shell plants all over the States were using our pH analyzers—nor was it any of our traditional competitors. It was a Dutch company we had never heard of by the name of Electrofact. From the looks of the company's data sheets, its engineers had to be wearing green eye shades and sleeve garters. It was easy to see why it hadn't sold anything outside of Holland.

This Shell chief instrumentation engineer had never even seen a UNI-LOC pH analyzer. So I offered him a free trial. He said he didn't have time to fool around with evaluations. He had made up his mind, and he didn't want to be bothered.

Finally, after lunch in the executive dining room, I said to him, "You know, I really didn't have to come all the way to Holland to be insulted. I could've managed that at home." With that I bid him farewell. I later told Van Hengel not to worry, we weren't dead yet. Over the years I have learned to respect the "fat lady": It ain't over until she sings. Even though Rotterdam was the home of Royal Dutch Shell, I thought we might have an outside chance to backtrack through our Shell friends in the States, where we were highly regarded. It was a long shot and it did work to some extent. I have no idea of what the infighting must have been like within the Shell organization, but about three months later Van Hengel got part of that order for analyzers.

The Van Hengel Company of the Netherlands was the only sales representative company I came across in Europe, or the U.K., in the early 1970s that didn't manufacture its own products and that operated in a similar fashion to reps in the States. Cor van Hengel was very well-educated technically; he was personable and spoke impeccable English, as many Dutch do. He also had some very capable assistants. It would have been sweet had I been able to find another four reps just like him.

Perhaps you are wondering if we ever lost any big orders or contracts, since I have only talked about those we won. After we broke down the engineering-constructor barriers, we didn't lose many orders. And those we did lose were to our good friend and licensee Foxboro (after the demise of our largest competitor). We never lost a cooling water control system order, since we had no competition. We held a lovely monopoly for a long time.

Of course we knew that the day would come when we would get competition, that someone would find a way around our patents. We just kept prospecting for new markets, new products, and new applications, utilizing our sales rep network toward that end. The UNI-LOC of today has a much broader product line and an expanded market.

CHAPTER FIFTEEN
IN CONCLUSION

When we were within a few months of the end of the earn-out period, I was told that if I wanted to make Betz a career I could have a seat on its board and continue running UNI-LOC as long as I wanted. It was mighty tempting because of my feelings for the Betz people, but I had other fish to fry. My wife and I wanted out of California in the worst way because of the smog and the overcrowded conditions. We had already made plans to move as soon as the earn-out period was over. In keeping with my long-standing habit of being ahead of the curve instead of behind it, I had already chosen my successor as UNI-LOC's president some time ago. I just hadn't gotten around to telling Betz. Of course, the decision was ultimately theirs, but I was confident they would accept my recommendation. My choice was Phil Cardeiro.

At that time, Phil had more maturity and business smarts than any of our other founders. He was deficient in the sales area, but he had lived with me long enough to understand that he needed the best possible sales support. And with Frova, he

had one of the best in sales. Phil was tough, but fair. And he had
the best overall grasp of a high-tech manager's role. Betz accepted
my recommendation. Cardeiro became UNI-LOC's second president upon my retirement in 1972.

By the time the earn-out period finally ended, UNI-LOC's
profits before taxes had increased by more than 150 percent,
and Betz made out exceptionally well. We left a lot of money on
the table, but then we did get our 100 percent stock bonus. Entering this new two-year restriction period found the stock once
again poised for a split. Betz certainly held up its end of the
bargain with its exemplary performances, and UNI-LOC's profits really helped. As you would expect, we had a gigantic cele-
bration—and this time the champagne was Dom Perignon.

So What Happened to the UNI-LOC Gang?

Was this the end of our personal relationships? Not by a long
shot. Our lives remained intertwined in many ways over the
ensuing years. Four of us—Barben, Cardeiro, Coombe, and I—
had several diverse investments together, some of which are
still in place today. We ran the gamut, or the gauntlet, investing
in land, income properties, oil and gas exploration, cattle, and
variations thereof. About the only thing we missed were rail-
road cars. We made money on most and we lost on some. And
we learned that "sophisticated investor" can be a fancy euphe-
mism for "sucker." But overall we made more than we lost.

Cardeiro, Barben, Horner, and Coombe all stayed on with
UNI-LOC after I left. "Boomer" Coomber remained as comptroller for about ten years following the earn-out. And he was
the mainstay when Betz sold UNI-LOC.

It really was no surprise that shortly after Cardeiro, Horner, and Barben left—which was about four years after my retirement—Betz sold UNI-LOC to Rosemont Laboratories, a subsidiary of Emerson Electric, a Fortune 500 company. With four of the five UNI-LOC top managers gone, Betz looked at itself and decided it was first and foremost a chemical company. It would continue to use UNI-LOC instruments, but it no longer wanted to manufacture them.

Eldon Means, from our original group of five, had elected to take cash and bail out of UNI-LOC at the time of the Betz acquisition; he didn't participate in the earn-out. Eldon was weary of the routine and wanted to go prospecting for gold, and the last we heard he was doing just that in South America. I know he was the only partner who wasn't using his strongest aptitudes at UNI-LOC, which is why, unlike the rest of us, he often experienced work frustrations. Had he elected to stay with UNI-LOC through the earn-out I would have insisted that he be tested by the Human Engineering Lab to see where within the company he could have been fulfilled. It has been several years since any of us have heard from Eldon so we can only assume he was successful and didn't return to the States. Had he come home I'm sure that one of the partners would have heard from him.

Following three years as UNI-LOC's second president, Phil Cardeiro decided to leave electronics engineering and cater to his other passion—Oriental fine art, mainly ancient dynasty pottery and rare jewelry. It didn't take him long to establish himself among the recognized experts of the world. He even developed a method for authenticating jade, much to the consternation of a few well-known dealers in that commodity. He also established his Art-Asia Museum in the Pebble Beach area of California. This is typical of the genuine entrepreneur: He grew bored with the same old game, wanted to expand his interests and education, as well as his horizons. Cardeiro and I have remained in touch over the years.

Jack Horner stayed with Betz–UNI-LOC about one year after the earn-out. He always loved the good life and those lean UNI-LOC years were real penance for him. Being a free spirit he was a handful to manage, but he held up well and did his part no matter what was required. When the Betz earn-out period was over, Jack indulged his old passion for fine cars, promptly buying a Ferrari and a Rolls Royce, as well as a 65-foot twin diesel motor yacht, which he christened the "Blue Heron," as well as a new home in Newport Beach. Self-denial was not Jack's hallmark and he had been penned up long enough.

Jack used to love to tell this story about himself, which is a tribute to his incredible sense of humor. (His capacity to see a humorous side to every setback we had at UNI-LOC was a welcome tonic.) When Jack was in college in the early 1950s, he raced sports cars as a hobby, those early British MGs and Jaguar XKs. Following graduation from Carnegie Tech, Jack decided to open a foreign car agency in Pittsburgh and, with his dad's help, he did. (Jack's father, also a chemist, owned a company that manufactured food colorings for the dairy industry. Horner was born with a bit of a golden spoon.) He also continued racing to advertise his agency, which sold sports cars, including Jaguars and MGs, and also nonracing cars, such as the Morris Minor and the Hillman Minx. He also had one of the very first VW Bugs to come to America. Horner sold a lot of cars:

Sports cars were the latest avant-garde toys at that time and Morris Minors were cheap transportation for those on the opposite end of the pecking order.

But nobody ever bought the Bug. It was painted a sort of olive drab with surplus woolen German Army uniform material for upholstery; while the quality was very good, the appearance was just plain ugly. Everyone who came into the show room wanted to drive it, and did. And everyone loved the way it handled—but no one would buy it. This went on for a year, until one day Jack got fed up and sold the car to his service manager at cost; then he sold his five-state VW distributorship, again to his service manager, for $25. No joke. Remember, this was some time before the Bug began to catch on. But you can imagine how Jack felt a couple of years later—after he had sold the sports car dealership and settled down as a chemical engineer—when the Bug became a cult car. Talk about being in the right place at the wrong time. There must be a lesson in there someplace, but I can't find it.

The last time I saw Jack Horner was at a bon voyage party on the Blue Heron. He had loaded his family aboard and was taking off for the Panama Canal en route to the Bahamas. He made it okay and stayed in Caribbean waters for a long time. By the time he returned to Orange County, I had already moved to Nevada. Our paths never crossed again. The last word I had was that Jack Horner had passed away a couple of years ago. His life was shorter than it should have been but he got more out of it than most people. I have always been pleased that UNI-LOC was the platform that made it possible for him to once again achieve some of the good life he so enjoyed.

Wes Coombe remained with UNI-LOC for several years following the departure of Means, Cardeiro, Barben, Horner, and myself, and through Rosemont-Emerson's acquisition of UNI-LOC from Betz. He continued to work until he was seventy-five, the year he shot his age in golf. Boomer was the best golfing buddy I ever had, and when my family and I moved to Nevada I didn't play golf for three years (although my wife and I made up for it later). I joined a bunch of the old NLS and UNI-LOC gangs on Boomer's 75th birthday for one of our "good old days golf tournaments," where, I am proud to say I won (following a disastrous three over on the combined first and second holes, but managing even par on 3 through 18). But the 19th hole was always our favorite and we had a blast. By then I had fully recovered from Scotland.

Wes and his wife spend most of their time on cruise ships or trains or boating down the Amazon or some such thing. Every year he sends us a half-dozen thick documentaries describing every facet of their trips, laced with Boomer Coomber humor. As I see it, the only problem Wes and Bernice have is trying to decide where to go next. He recently authored *Travel by George* (published by Xlibris Corp.). George Wescoombe is his pen name and old Boomer has never been funnier.

Restless Guns

Ted Barben had stayed with UNI-LOC as vice president for about three years after the earn-out. When our noncompetition agreements expired, I talked him into moving to Carson City, Nevada. For the first year he just dinked around building a house and playing with hydroponic gardening. He grew some dandy tomatoes. (I think for a while he was considering the commercial possibilities.) For the previous four years I, too, had done little other than spend time with my kids, who were in high school at the time, building a small aviation-related business at the Carson City airport and building a home, doing my own finish carpentry. Besides thirty-five rental aircraft hangars, I built a 10,000 square-foot manufacturing facility peripheral to the airport and with airport access. I rented half to a machine shop and used the other half as my personal hangar and hobby shop.

One day Barben said he had a new idea for a pH reference cell that he thought would be a patentable improvement to the one I had designed for UNI-LOC, the one using the wood plug as a liquid junction.

Barben's new reference cell was a mechanical device with an *internal wood maze*, vacuum-impregnated with potassium chloride electrolyte. The advantage of this cell over UNI-LOC's was that it lasted five to ten times longer between replenishment cycles; that is, it seldom had to be recharged with silver chloride, perhaps once every year or eighteen months. It would be much more convenient to use, but a bit more costly—and well worth it.

I agreed it had patent possibilities, and asked him what he wanted to do. He suggested we build a prototype to see how it works, then decide if we want to sell the patent to UNI-LOC or build and sell the reference cells ourselves. I had plenty of spare room in my factory-hangar, so we set up a little R&D area and for the next few weeks Barben worked on the cell.

After perfecting the new reference cell, the question was what to do with it. We didn't like the idea of selling it outright to another company or of licensing it because then we would have no control over sales and marketing. And because licensing would mean that royalties would be paid to us based on sales, we wanted control over sales.

But should we produce only reference cells and try to lure customers into buying our cells over those supplied by the pH analyzer manufacturers? We could do this on an aftermarket basis, but it would be next to impossible to do on initial analyzer sales. Moreover, it would be a slow and tedious process to build a company strictly on the aftermarket. The next logical question was, do we also design and build a pH analyzer to go with our revolutionary reference cells and then go head-to-head with UNI-LOC, Foxboro, or whomever else was out there?

That called for some heavy-duty thinking. The idea of starting from scratch and competing with our own marvelous creation, UNI-LOC, didn't really appeal to us. The thought of building another national sales representative organization sure as hell didn't appeal to me. And another thing, could we build a good pH analyzer without infringing on UNI-LOC's patent, which had been validated in court against the company that ended up paying treble damages? We certainly wanted no part of anything like that. And where in northern Nevada could we find another Phil Cardeiro to design the electronics for a new pH analyzer? In 1976, Carson City wasn't exactly a high-tech center. Electronic engineers were nonexistent. As an example, when Ted applied to the Nevada State Board to accept his California chemical P.E. license, he was issued a Nevada license with the serial number 001.

In reviewing the UNI-LOC patent and the court findings, Ted rediscovered something we had forgotten. All of UNI-LOC's patent claims had been disallowed, based upon their being "obvious,"in the judge's uninformed opinion, to those trained in the art. The only claim that had survived had to do with matching the natural impedance of the FET pre-amplifier with the glass electrode in the presence of temperature changes of the fluids being measured. This was a result of the way Cardeiro had designed and mounted the pre-amp. And that single claim is what hung the defendant and resulted in those enormous treble damages.

Remember earlier when I said that in a rapidly changing high-tech world such as ours, sooner or later somebody would discover a different way to "skin the cat?" Little did I dream that we would be doing the skinning. But, in truth, the UNI-LOC patent had been decimated by a dumb judge.

We hired a patent attorney to confirm our findings and concluded that we could, indeed, design a new pH analyzer. It would do everything the UNI-LOC analyzer would do, except we wouldn't have that inherent impedance matching capability because we would handle our electrode pre-amplification in a different way. But we could externally compensate for temperature changes if needs be. This would completely avoid any conflict with the UNI-LOC patent.

So we decided to explore the idea of designing and producing our own pH analyzer along with the new Barben reference cell. We then figured we needed a company entity of some sort, with all the protection we could get, so we incorporated our new little enterprise under the name Thomas–Barben Instruments, soon to be known as TBI. Ted proceeded with his patent application while I made some production configuration drawings of the new pH reference cell.

We set out to find an electronic consulting engineer who could design the latest state-of-the-art circuitry for our new analyzer. Just for the heck of it, I called Phil Cardeiro to see if he was remotely interested in joining us, but he declined for three reasons. He loved the Pebble Beach area. He was firmly established in his ancient Oriental art business. And he felt the electronics industry had leaped so forward in the areas of microcircuits and chips during his absence that he would have to spend too much time getting up to speed. It just wasn't worth it to him. I even brought him out to northern Nevada and flew him around our Carson City/Reno/Lake Tahoe area in hopes of enticing him, but no dice. Had he been a skier we might have lured him. We were three years too late to get Phil.

Ted finally settled on a California consultant, and we began to prepare for the debut of the newest entrant into the pH analyzer business. Refinements on the new reference cell were being made and I made a series of design layouts for how we wanted the new analyzer to look. We decided to stay with inert plastics throughout and avoid metals as much as possible, especially in our enclosures. Again, simplicity was the object. We had enough experience to know what the industry would accept and what it wouldn't.

That first electronic consultant didn't work out, so we had to look around for another who could deliver on schedule. It was a long time before the puzzle pieces came together into a marketable device. While Ted spent his time fine-tuning the analyzer and the reference cell, I began thinking about a sales rep organization. UNI-LOC, of course, had the best reps in the business for pH equipment and I had no reason to think any of them were dissatisfied. However, I decided to contact a couple of them anyway and test the waters. I was surprised to find that the Van London Company of Houston, Texas, which had been my number one rep, was having a feud with UNI-LOC and would be delighted to make a change—especially if it meant being re-affiliated with Barben and me. Ted and I decided that we would only establish one rep for the time being, and do our market testing through Van London on the Gulf Coast before trying to support more reps. We knew we would be making some special accommodations and changes, and we thought it better to have all the technical modifications and additions made before spreading our wings nationally. Good thinking. And truthfully, I was getting a bit lazy. Ted, however, unlike me, didn't have any other interests or hobbies—and besides, he was a lot younger. Ever since I've known him his life has been consumed by the technical challenges of high-tech enterprises. The term "workaholic" was coined with Ted Barben in mind.

Deja Vu

I just didn't want to go through the exercise of establishing a national rep organization by myself again, unless I couldn't find anyone else to do it. Who in the world could I get to take my place in sales and marketing for TBI? Ted and I had been at it by ourselves for more than a year, so we weren't surrounded by a reservoir of versatile talent like we had been at UNI-LOC. I couldn't borrow somebody from engineering and put him in specialty sales, as I had done with Ted and Carl Frova. And there was no way I would consider bringing a stranger in for such a vital position—no matter how highly recommended. I had to have a known quantity, and I was prepared to pay the price with TBI ownership. And if that didn't work, I would do it myself. One way or the other it would get done.

Although Barben and I were both in a strong financial condition, unlike when we started UNI-LOC, and even though we could have afforded to pay handsome salaries to get people to move to Nevada and join TBI, we decided to structure and operate TBI just as we had UNI-LOC. None of this business of hiring guys and paying big salaries and expecting them to bust their butts like we do. Only ownership generates that kind of activity, so, just like UNI-LOC, the key people must be owners. After comparing the talents of several candidates with whom I had worked, I decided there was only one man for the job—and that was Bob Anderson, my old UNI-LOC rep in Detroit, Michigan. Bob had been my inside sales coordinator at NLS, and later became an independent NLS and UNI-LOC rep in Detroit. He had spent a lot of time with me in the field and was the best student of sales I ever had. I had to get him. Ted concurred, and between the two of us we reserved an attractive block of TBI stock for Bob—if he would join us.

Since we would be operating TBI the same way we had run UNI-LOC, the key people would own stock, but would receive no salaries until we were profitable enough to pay them. The same would hold true for Bob Anderson if he decided to accept our offer and move to Nevada. When I called Bob, he told me he had to fly out to San Diego on NLS business, and suggested that Barben and I meet him there, which we did. Ted and I outlined our plans to Bob and he was quite interested, mainly I think because of his past affiliation with us. However, he knew nothing about northern Nevada and wanted to bring his wife and daughters for a visit to see if all would be compatible. Bob's wife was a psychiatric nurse, and she was offered a good teaching job at Carson City Community College. Bob sold his substantial rep business in Detroit to his number one associate on a buyout basis, which turned out well for both parties. Their home sold quickly, and within three months of the San Diego meeting Bob Anderson had joined TBI as vice president of sales and marketing—and as a shareholder.

Bob, who was better known as Andy, was another character and a half. When I first met him back at NLS, he was fresh out of the Navy where he had been an electronics technician. He was my best student of professional sales and developed into one of the best sales engineers in the business.

By now, Barben and I had been at it for almost two years. I had decided I would stay with TBI only until it was well enough launched to ensure that a successful outcome was probable. I thought that this wouldn't take long—and it didn't! It was mutually agreed that I would sell my TBI interest equally to both Ted and Bob. Although the company was still small, with only one full-time paid employee, there was no question that it was only a matter of time and it would be rock solid. The product was excellent and Anderson was doing a terrific job establishing a rep organization. TBI rented my building for three more years, at which time Bob and Ted bought it; within two more years they doubled its size. TBI was firmly launched. At the time it was one of only a handful of genuine high-tech companies in northern Nevada.

Another Earn-out

It was fun to watch Barben and Anderson apply the UNI-LOC management principles and structure to TBI as it grew and as they added key people at critical times. They made sure their prime movers were shareholders and consequently they never lost anyone. Company loyalty was first rate. Nevertheless, several years later the time came when both Andy and Ted, for different reasons, decided to sell. They patiently sought a compatible marriage partner, which turned out to be one of the oldest and most respected names in liquid process instrumentation—Bailey Controls, a subsidiary of McDermott, a Fortune 500 company. They worked out an earn-out program with Bailey similar to the one we had when Betz acquired UNI-LOC. All the key TBI people remained through the earn-out period, which was a couple of years, during which time their holdings increased substantially.

Where is TBI today? Still in Carson City, but no longer known as TBI. It has now been in business for more than twenty-five years and is a division of the giant Swiss conglomerate ABB.

Like UNI-LOC before it, TBI was about as fail-proof as a company can be. So we had two start-ups that developed into businesses that were acquired by Fortune 500 companies. Not bad. I think we've proven our point about how to fund, structure, and manage "The Fail-Proof Enterprise."

Bob Anderson decided he wanted to retire to his boyhood homeland in the Upper Peninsula of Michigan, which he did, playing ice hockey in the winter and golf in the summer. He often joined Boomer and me for golf in the old NLS and UNI-LOC days, and he was at Boomer's 75th birthday golf bash.

What about Barben? He'll never know when to quit. Not long after his separation from TBI he got a bug about air pollution abatement and developed a gas analyzer for detecting and recording levels of toxic gases emanating from industrial smoke stacks. Needless to say, his latest enterprise is in concert with the objectives of the Environmental Protection Agency. His company, Universal Analyzers, is also located in the Carson City Industrial Airpark; it is now several years old—and very successful. His newest product fresh out of development is yet another revolutionary pH reference cell with companion electronics.

Universal Analyzers has just completed its second engineering and manufacturing facility. Business is booming, and there is no doubt about the potential longevity of this company. One of these days I'm sure Ted will work out an earn-out program with another Fortune 500 company and make it three for three. The other day at lunch I asked him why he keeps his nose to the grindstone: He works at least ten hours a day. His answer was, "Bob, you know my life is my work. This is what I have to do. And besides, I'm unemployable." That said it all.

I couldn't argue with him. When asked why I hadn't remained as president of UNI-LOC following the Betz earn-out, I have two honest answers: (1) It had been more than a year since anybody had asked me a question I hadn't heard before, and (2) I was unemployable and I knew it. No matter how much I liked and respected the Betz people, I could never have adjusted to bureaucratic, corporate political gamesmanship, and sooner or later that is what it comes down to. In both UNI-LOC and TBI none of us had the time nor the inclination for the political power games that run rampant in bureaucratic institutions.

All of us veteran entrepreneurs are unemployable over the long term. Once you have owned your own soul, game-playing by other people's rules is no longer possible. There is no turning back.

EPILOGUE

So how do I feel about all that has happened? Looking back is something new to me. I have always been too busy trying to get the most out of today and looking forward to tomorrow to give much thought to yesterday. I know that I would never have written this book had it not been for that gnawing in my gut to share my knowledge and experience with *somebody*, to share what I know about creating a fail-proof enterprise when you don't have much money.

Writing this book has forced me to look back. And I like what I see. I am proud to have been part of the creation of two living, vibrant companies and to have been associated with outstanding partners and key employees who never lost sight of our goals. What were our goals? To create, produce, and market the finest products of their kinds. Technical excellence! We reached our goals, and lots of money was the result. Money, however, was never our conscious goal.

Before I close, however, I want to reinforce a few points that are vitally important to the creation of a fail-proof enterprise.

The first is to know your attributes and respect your limitations. Earlier I mentioned the aptitude tests I took at the Human Engineering Laboratory.* I took those tests when I was at a crossroads. I wasn't sure what I wanted to do. Those tests, and the follow-up counseling the Lab offered, helped me discover my strengths. This is crucial to your success. There is no sense spending your life trying to make the shoe fit if it doesn't. Find out what you do best and do it. And leave the rest by the wayside.

Please note that I have no connection whatsoever with the Human Engineering Laboratory. In fact, I have not had contact with them, except to order data sheets, for more than twenty years. Furthermore, the Lab knows nothing about this book and they may not agree with some of what I have to say. I am writing solely about my own personal experiences with Lab testing.

As I have said several times, and I cannot stress it enough, it takes good partners to make a good business. And there are two "musts" in any successful partnership: Aptitude compatibility and vocabulary compatibility.

In a partnership, it is essential that the managing partners' strongest aptitudes be complementary; they should dovetail, not conflict. Ideally, you want each person within the enterprise to be performing different tasks extremely well. But you want similarity in vocabulary level: Everyone's must be high. At the

---

*Human Engineering Laboratory, Inc., 347 Beacon Street, Boston, MA 02116. There are branch offices in Atlanta, Chicago, Dallas/Ft. Worth, Denver, Houston, Los Angeles, New York, San Francisco, Seattle, and Washington, D.C.

management level, low-vocabulary people and high-vocabulary people cannot get along in the long run. The low-vocabulary person will run out of words and become frustrated, and communication breaks down.

However, with some dedication, vocabulary can be easily improved. The Human Engineering Lab has a wonderful vocabulary-building program called "Wordbook," which consists of eight booklets. Now the idea is not to use big words to impress others, as does, say, William F. Buckley, Jr., who delights in using his immense vocabulary as a rapier. Vocabulary is knowledge, pure and simple. It is imperative that business managers accurately comprehend what they hear and what they read. And college graduate vocabulary levels are no longer good enough.

My sons and daughters were tested as teenagers, and they never had any problems in college. One graduated summa cum laude, another Phi Beta Kappa, and another with high honors. And they all carefully structured their careers around their strongest aptitudes. If I have learned nothing else in life, I have learned that working and playing (hobbies) within one's strongest aptitudes is a *must* for obtaining excellent results with less effort and long-term *emotional stability.*

Forewarned is forearmed! Know everything you can about your strengths and weaknesses and let your competitors guess at theirs. Aptitude testing, such as that offered by the Human Engineering Laboratory, is the best assurance you can have that you—meaning you and your partners—are maximizing your collective management abilities.

Corporate Responsibility?

We hear so much about this thing called "corporate responsibility." I am from the old school and I totally reject sociologists and psychologists telling corporate leaders that we have social and financial obligations to our respective communities over and above providing good jobs and paying taxes. However, I do believe we corporate leaders have a moral obligation to provide our employees with the best possible salaries, safe working conditions, and job security. And we must stand behind them as long as we possibly can in times of emergency or business slowdown. If we are to survive together, we must function as a family. This comes down to basic human decency and responsibility. Nothing fancy about it.

I personally will never hold still for behavioral types who try to make me feel guilty because I refuse to set up internal mechanisms that would make it easier for groups to get their hands in our corporate or our employees' pockets.

That said, I have to acknowledge the other side of the coin: the selfish and greedy behavior practiced by the majority of entrepreneurs I have known. In the early stages of a new enterprise, those involved are usually humble, awed, and just grateful for the chance to make it happen. Then, as the company grows and becomes profitable and they build up their reserves, the owners begin to get a taste of affluence. Humility disappears, only to be replaced by an avarice of increasing proportions. And when the company finally prospers in a big way, the owners focus more and more on material excesses at the expense of remembering how they got their golden opportunities in the first place. Getting back to Herzberg and his thesis about

money being a "dissatisfier," no entrepreneur is ever completely satisfied with however much money he or she may accumu-
late. It is contrary to human nature not to want just a little more,
you know, for a rainy day.

What I ask entrepreneurs to consider is the big picture.
Where did you come from? What circumstances made it possible
for you to have the opportunity to do what you have done? The
answer, of course, is our private enterprise system. That is what
made it all possible. Nothing else. Am I waving the flag as the
finale for this book? Not intentionally. I am merely stating a fact.

What you entrepreneurs have to do is give back part of
yourselves to the system that allows you to become what you
are. I am talking about entering the world of politics and public
service, either on a part-time or full-time basis, *and give our
nation some genuine leadership for a refreshing change.* If we don't
begin *now* to prevent more activist public sector lawyers, well-
born liberals, and retired public employee tax-takers from continuing to dominate our national and state elected offices, we
will lose our private enterprise system—and all the future
opportunities that could be borne from it. Government and private partnerships are counterproductive, but that is what we
will have more of if entrepreneurs don't drastically change the
make-up of our lawmaking bodies.

Oh, I know, who wants to go into politics? Least of all we
freewheeling entrepreneurs. After all, politics is beneath our
dignity, right? Well, this may surprise you but when I retired
from my business career I did so to enter politics and public
service. Why? Because I had always wanted to? Hell no! I did it
because I didn't feel right about making more money when I

really had enough. Yes, I felt guilty about being a taker and not a giver to the "system" that allowed me to be what I am. Until that time, I had never considered any kind of elective office. I was the antithesis of what a politician is perceived to be. I have never been a rah-rah guy or a glad-hander. I don't kiss babies and I'm not particularly friendly. But I felt compelled to give it a try anyway. I ran first for our local school board: I won and served four years. Following that, I worked to get myself appointed by the governor to the Nevada State Welfare Board, where I served three years in an advisory capacity. And then I ran for the Nevada legislature against a firmly entrenched incumbent and was narrowly defeated. Did it tear me up to lose, to be rejected? We entrepreneurs aren't used to having our egos tweaked. And it wasn't as bad as losing a contract. Two years later I tried again and won. I served as a state assemblyman for three terms and could have remained there to this day had I wanted to, but I believe in term limits, and by then *I had paid my dues*. It was time for another private enterpriser to take my place but, alas, there were no private enterprisers who would try.

Did I accomplish anything cosmic as a lawmaker? Maybe yes and maybe no, depending on who you talk to. But I was instrumental in harpooning a lot of potentially rotten legislation. My reputation was that of being the best floor debater in the Assembly, and I capitalized on it every chance I got. But sadly, I was mostly alone. Just think what might have been accomplished had I had a few business leader types in there with me. Of the sixty-three legislators, not counting ranchers, there were only two business people in the Assembly, where my party was outnumbered two-to-one, and only two businessmen in the Senate where, again, my party was in the minority. Was it a worthwhile experience to have served in the legislature? Absolutely! It was an introspective experience, and I am a much better man for having done it. And for the first time, I came to truly understand how and why government is driven to infringe on our economic freedoms as established by our forefathers *unless we entrepreneurs stop it*. There is no alternative.

Can this long trend be reversed? Yes. But *only* when those of us who truly understand private enterprise and free markets, those of us who have created a private enterprise with our own hands, begin the slow process of reshaping the lawmaking ideologies of our federal and state governments. Sadly, all other options are merely delaying tactics. What more rewarding way can there be for an entrepreneur to top-off a career than by offering hardwon leadership and problem-solving skills, aided by intuitive and learned abilities to understand the big picture, in guiding our country toward increasing economic freedom and prosperity? Believe me, it is exciting. Think about it.

It is time to bring down the curtain on the UNI-LOC story. Everything you have read here about our experiences in that exciting enterprise is fact. (Although I have omitted several individuals' names and company names for obvious reasons, believe me, I remember them all.) It is true, we had some good luck: We were in the right place at the right time and we had a superbly patient and understanding first customer in Ma Bell. But in the final analysis our success must be attributed to a lot of hard work and some ingenuity, coupled with exceptionally talented and dedicated personnel who were in the right slots— because we understood what our strengths were—*and a bullet-*

proof company structure. We had some setbacks and a few frustrations but we could have survived much worse.

I realize that the claim of having created the "fail-proof enterprise" is a big one, but I believe with all my heart and my mind that if you have good products and/or services, and you structure and manage your company the same way we structured and managed UNI-LOC, it will be as fail-proof as it is humanly possible to be. I wish you the best.

THE TEN ESSENTIALS
OF THE FAIL-PROOF ENTERPRISE

In the preceding chapters you have seen the innovative policies that laid the foundation for UNI-LOC's success as "The Fail-Proof Enterprise" in practice. True, we created products that were outstanding. Had we been unsuccessful in that effort, we would not have continued past the gestation period. We would never have risked bankruptcy. As I have said repeatedly: Outstanding products or uniquely dedicated services are the first requisites for success.

Some of the following Ten Essentials were original to me and UNI-LOC, and some were acquired from my previous employers. All are important, albeit some more than others. However, over time, as your enterprise gains momentum, if I were you I would make every effort to incorporate all ten essentials into my business. With all ten in place your enterprise will be as fail-proof as it could possibly be. And assuming you pay decent wages, it will be a peaceful and highly valued place to work for your employees. You will then have every possible advantage over your competitors.

ESSENTIAL #1
All Owner–Participants Should Be Tested
to Determine their Attributes and Limitations.

Assuming you have decided on the products or services to be offered by your new company and that you have, tentatively at least, selected your partners and associates, it is imperative that you and your owner–management group identify your collective abilities. I strongly recommend that all potential owner–managers be tested by the Human Engineering Laboratory, which has been in business for over eighty years.

I can't think of anything more important—other than the quality and uniqueness of your products—than being sure your key people have diverse, but complementary, aptitudes. If I were forming a new company today, I would not have anyone as a member of the owner–management group whose *strongest* aptitude did not differ from those of the other owners. This paves the way for nonconflicting relationships.

Each partner should be given primary responsibility for the aspect of the business that best matches his or her highest aptitude. We all have had an experience where our innate abilities were not put to their best use: This is a principal cause of job unrest and frustration. You do not want that situation in your company. Ideally, the partners will also have secondary abilities that will enable them to pinch-hit in other departments as necessary.

Acquired skills are important, but without inborn natural abilities to back up those learned skills, you and your partners will fall short as your company evolves. The owner–managers should be able to provide as wide a variety of usable skills as possible. This will enable your enterprise to remain an entrepreneurship much longer.

This next point may be difficult to accept but it is vital to the success of your enterprise. You need to determine whether you, as the principal entrepreneur, have the attributes to be the leader, the managing director. If you have the wrong "personality" aptitude, you will fail miserably as a manager—and your company will fail. It may be necessary for you to appoint another partner CEO, president, or general manager—the general manager must be a natural-born "people person." You can still be chairman of the board, principal owner, or policy director. Do not let ego get in the way of building a strong foundation for your business.

Another major consideration is vocabulary. According to the Human Engineering Lab, low-vocabulary people don't stand a chance of becoming successful managers in worthwhile enterprises. *Vocabulary is knowledge*—and you and your core owner–management group must have broad knowledge. Again, this is not some way to flaunt supposed "superiority." A high-level vocabulary is an important business tool: To be an effective owner–manager, you must be able to understand the nuances of what is said to you and of what you read. In fact, according to the Lab, successful corporation presidents consistently outscore college presidents in vocabulary tests.

Communication is key in developing a successful business. Low-vocabulary people become frustrated and angry when they cannot express themselves, or cannot understand what is being said. They blow up, they storm out of meetings. And when a low-vocabulary person is the principal owner, that enterprise's days are numbered. The low-vocabulary owner will alienate and ultimately lose key people.

Can anything be done about a low-level vocabulary? Of course, and very simply with some daily dedication to study. The Human Engineering Lab has one of the best vocabulary-building programs available, and most colleges and universities offer courses. As I have said, in today's information age, a college-level vocabulary is no longer good enough.

ESSENTIAL #2
Don't Pay Salaries to Yourselves Initially.
Issue Stock in Lieu of Salaries.

I recognize that every business start-up is unique in some way. It may be that your particular industry requires huge investments in equipment at the outset—if you are going to manufacture automobiles, for example, or make millions of pairs of jeans. UNI-LOC was lucky in that the electronics manufacturing business doesn't usually require such an outlay. There are scores of electronic job shops that manufacture completed circuit boards to specifications if, and when, your quantities justify farming the work out. We were essentially a design-engineering, final-assembly, and test shop. Our biggest outlay was for test equipment and assembly tools—and that wasn't that large an amount. However, if you have no choice but to spend large sums in the beginning, then you may have to borrow, sell stock, or seek venture capital. But if you and your partners can possibly raise suffi-

cient capital among yourselves and make no-interest loans to
the venture, then by all means do it that way.

Once having raised the seed money, use it only for equipment and operating expenses. *Do not pay salaries.* You will only
be kidding yourselves if you do. Instead, the owner–managers
should work for a specified period of time—with UNI-LOC it
was eighteen months—without income, living off savings or
assets, in exchange for company stock. This allows the company to build up its cash reserves, and it gives the owner–managers the security of knowing they are shareholders right from
the beginning. No pie-in-the-sky promises. Living off savings
is by far the best way to keep the true financial condition of a
new venture in front of every participant. Believe me, their
spouses will remind them daily so you and your accountant
won't have to.

Make a formal agreement among yourselves as to share distribution. This will be influenced by several factors as it was with
UNI-LOC. However, the stock should not be issued until after
the no-salary period is over. You don't want any owner–partners
pledging their stock for a personal loan in order to exist without
a salary or for any other reason. You want partners who have a
track record of personal financial prudence: people who can sustain themselves through the gestation period without a salary, or
who are willing to refinance or sell their homes, put their spouses to work, or sell other assets as necessary. If he or she can get an
outside personal loan, that's okay, too—as long as company stock
isn't pledged as security. What I am talking about here is "total
commitment." And with that level of commitment you are more
than halfway to becoming a fail-proof company.

Under no circumstances can you allow company stock to accrue to outsiders who will never contribute anything to the operational well-being of the enterprise. Make a written agreement to that effect. The promise of stock or options at some future time is not good enough. You cannot expect to get a total, long-term commitment based on promises. What you will get is dissension. Remember, you don't want to end up owning 100 percent of a failure. You want a lesser percentage of success.

ESSENTIAL #3
Give Majority Ownership Collectively to Your Partners.

I cannot overemphasize the importance of giving your partners— collectively—at least 51 percent of the stock in the new enterprise. (Obviously, you won't do this if you have only one partner.) This should not be done in the beginning, however. Before relinquishing any control you must be certain that you have all the owner–managers you will need.

This may be another tough pill to swallow, but put yourself in your partners' shoes. If, as you, they are living off their savings during the start-up phase, and perhaps even putting some money in the pool for equipment and operations, then they have totally committed themselves to the effort. It isn't fair, or smart, to lock your partners into a minority voting situation. What if, for example, you become incapacitated, and your heirs try to take over the operation of the business? Your partners need the assurance that they collectively will have the power to keep things as they are—and to protect their investments and commitments to the company. If you have carefully selected your partners, if individually and collectively you trust their judgment, you should not fear being outvoted on policies or other weighty management decisions because that will only happen if you are dead wrong. I credit this single policy for the fact that we UNI-LOC partners had zero major disagreements during our entire tenure.

ESSENTIAL #4
Limit Your Organizational Structure
to Three Levels.

As I have mentioned many times throughout this book, a principal objective of the entrepreneurial enterprise, aside from business success, is to remain entrepreneurial. This is much easier said than done. Remember Thomas's First Law of Entrepreneurial Reality: *"If an enterprise continues to grow, at some point it will surely become a bureaucracy or will be acquired by a bureaucracy."* It's either that or fold the tent.

Again, why do we want to remain entrepreneurial? Because it is far more efficient, profitable, and fun than operating as a bureaucracy. And besides, when the time finally comes for you entrepreneurs to succumb to becoming "caretaker" managers in bureaucratically structured companies, you will find yourselves emotionally unsuited for the role.

By limiting the organizational structure of your enterprise to three levels—with top management functioning collectively as the policymaking body and functioning independently as departmental managers; with the lead-people forming the middle level; and with manufacturing, assembly, warehouse, maintenance, and other support people making up the bottom level —then all growth becomes horizontal. This makes it much easier to manage without resorting to paper-shuffling middle managers. Middle managers with titles like Director of Human Resources, Director of Materials, Chief Accountant, Chief Engineer, Manufacturing Manager, and so on, are the death knell of an entrepreneurship. They are the principal incubators of company politics and for that reason alone should be avoided for as long as possible.

The main advantage of the three-level company is that the traditional middle-management functions are handled by the top-level owner–managers with the support of the lead people in the middle level. No fancy power titles are needed—nor middle-management perks such as private offices, executive washrooms, and hot and cold running secretaries.

ESSENTIAL #5
Post Set Salary Levels.
No Time Clocks.

Establish and post salary levels, all the way up the ladder, and get rid of time clocks.

To maintain the highest level of employee morale avoid demeaning performance evaluations where employees are given obligatory, pittance raises. I submit that it is impossible to know that one employee is 25-cents-per-hour better than another. You will only make your employees angry because they know their raises are rote, *not earned*.

Establish salary levels that are not necessarily tied to specific tasks or job classifications, with incremental merit raises of at least $50 to $75 per week. If employees know what their next salary level will be, they have something to shoot for.

Time clocks make employees feel like peons who can't be trusted to get to work on time. And they can actually contribute to the problem they were meant to deter. Some employees think that because they will be docked for coming in late, their lateness shouldn't be a problem to management. Haven't they in effect paid for being late? (Never mind the added costs of the docking procedure.)

How do you handle tardiness problems if you don't have a time clock? First you must have the kind of company people want to work for. Then you must post your tardiness policy. Have a heart-to-heart talk with each employee, and tell each one flat-out that being late is irresponsible behavior that will not be tolerated. Make sure they realize that repeated tardiness or unexcused absences are reason for immediate termination. That's what we did at UNI-LOC and it worked just fine. I don't believe we fired more than one or two people and everyone else got the message.

That said, the best way to avoid those sorts of problems is to create a work environment that your employees value and won't want to lose. That is the best deterrent to irresponsible behavior.

ESSENTIAL #6
Establish Profit-Sharing.
Shut Down between Christmas
& New Year's Day With Pay.

Another great innovation that will make your employees want to stay in your employ is to set up an informal profit-sharing plan. Give everyone in the company the week off between Christmas and New Year's Day with pay, and distribute cash bonuses—if you can afford them—the day before the shut-down occurs. I say "informal" because you never want to be locked into an established, fixed profit-sharing policy; this can backfire if your company becomes unionized.

Every year we told our employees that the holiday vacation and bonuses were contingent upon our profitability up until December 1. By December 7, we would announce what would happen that year. At UNI-LOC we were always able to give our employees a week off with pay plus some cash, but it was never a foregone conclusion.

I was exposed to this idea at Northrop Aircraft Company. Management had found that very little work got done during the week between Christmas and New Year's anyway, so it was decided to make that time a paid vacation. Northrop was considered the premium aircraft company in Southern California to work for and that vacation was one reason. It also helped keep the company as the largest nonunion airframe company in the country. This type of profit-sharing is superior to the usual plans because it is highly visible—and it occurs at a sensitive and emotionally satisfying time of the year. The cash bonuses were the frosting on the cake. When you combine that five-day vacation with pay with the weekend preceding and the weekend following, you have up to nine consecutive days off. Time off and a cash bonus made it possible for our employees to really get into the Christmas spirit.

By the way, we did have a skeleton crew working that week and those employees received double pay.

ESSENTIAL #7
Maximize Your Profits in Anticipation
of the Time You Either Go Public or Sell.

You can't have it both ways. You cannot pay yourselves high salaries with benefits, plus bonuses, and then hope to command a high stock offering price when you decide to go public with your company's shares. The same holds true if you are thinking of selling out to another company or of merging. Another consideration is that bonuses are taxed as ordinary income, while share sales will be taxed at capital gains rates whether you go public or sell out. If your enterprise is highly profitable, denying yourselves big salaries and bonuses can be difficult for many entrepreneurs, especially after having worked hard for years to establish the company. You want some of the good life *now*—and that is understandable. But if you and your partners have collectively set a target end-date for going public or selling out, the waiting and denial will be less painful. You will know that by waiting just a little bit longer, you will likely profit fivefold—or more.

ESSENTIAL #8
Do Not Be Acquired without First
Negotiating an Earn-Out Program.

Unless you have made up your mind to take cash for your company or go public with your stock, under no circumstances should you take publicly traded shares in trade for your company unless you have an earn-out program that will allow you to protect the future value of those shares. There will be an SEC time restriction on the sale of any shares you take in trade, the reasoning being that once you "own" those shares, you are considered an "insider" in the (publicly traded) acquiring company. Although the Securities and Exchange Commission currently calls for a two-year moratorium, that could change at any time. It could become even longer than two years. And believe me, you have no idea how long two years can be until you begin watching the daily fluctuations in the share value of the stock you took in trade for your beloved company.

An earn-out program is no guarantee that the value of your shares will be protected against a downward slide. But if you can earn additional shares based upon *your company's continued performance*—say for a future period of two or three years—you would then be protected against a share value loss. We had a three-year earn-out, and if we doubled our profitability by the end of the three years, we would receive additional shares of stock equal to the number established when we made the deal—a 100 percent bonus. We figured that would at least insulate our original block of stock against a 50 percent loss in value over the two-year SEC restriction. As it turned out, because of our parent company's share price performance, which resulted in stock splits during that two-year restriction period, our stock value quadrupled before our earn-out period was concluded. During our second two-year SEC restriction period, on our new earn-out shares, the stock split again.

We were fortunate, but you never know what is going to happen. The important thing is to have a favorable earn-out program in place before your business is acquired by a publicly traded company.

ESSENTIAL #9
A CEO Should Take Time Each Week to
Visit with Individual Employees.

Entrepreneurial CEOs rarely have anything to do that is more important than getting to know their employees. Company parties or get-togethers don't cut the mustard because everyone is always on their best and most guarded behavior at those functions. Slipping on a pair of coveralls and sitting down at a workbench with assemblers or cutters or graphic artists or the bookkeeper or whomever, one at a time, spending fifteen minutes with each, maybe helping to assemble a part and all the while visiting about anything and everything, pays dividends you cannot believe until you have done it for some period of time. In later years I did this at UNI-LOC for a half day every Monday morning. We talked about sports, kids, cooking, boyfriends, girlfriends, husbands, wives—everything except business.

Of course, eventually there comes a physical limit to this wonderful pastime when the CEO may have to enlist the help of one of the other owner–managers. But for one-half day each week there should be a sufficient number of owner–managers on the factory floor with the employees to assure that every employee gets a visit once a month. The visit can take place standing by a machine, or helping out in the shipping department, or when grabbing a broom and sweeping out a factory area. It doesn't matter where you are or what you end up doing—as long as your employees can see that you are not above getting your hands dirty, and that you are willing to do whatever they do. This is also a sleeper in discovering hidden potential talents from the standpoint of sampling employee general knowledge, attitudes, values, interests, personality, and more. When employees are treated like the interesting real people they are, they will go the extra mile for the company.

ESSENTIAL #10
Open Your Office Space into
Friendly, Lively Bullpens.

Private offices are a waste of valuable space, incubators for wasted time and office politics, and symbols of management arrogance. More time is squandered behind closed office doors than in any factory or shop area. Private offices are supposed to be symbolic rewards of achievement, but your business isn't in the business of catering to individual egos. Cubicles, on the other hand, are the insult of insults to those trapped within, especially when they are all the same, lined up like neat little boxes. Ticky-tacky!

A properly designed, open-office bullpen is the epitome of efficiency. If liberally carpeted and outfitted with sound-deadening walls, and if the desks are spaced far enough apart, office personnel will not bother one another while doing their duties. Even phone conversations remain private.

The bullpen eliminates the office caste system. The president and vice presidents may have more space between their desks, but they are still out there for everyone to see and perhaps learn from by observation. With the bullpen layout, everyone usually knows where everyone else is, so no time is lost tracking someone down all over the facility. Communication is vastly improved because information can be more freely exchanged and misinformation more quickly corrected.

What happens when a company grows? Set up more than one bullpen by combining compatible departments, or have a bullpen for each department, if the company is big enough. The only private areas should be the conference room and a meeting room off each bullpen.

Final Comments

Is it possible to build a successful entrepreneurial enterprise without incorporating all of the Ten Essentials? Yes! It is possible to be successful in a number of ways, such as just being lucky. But why not be sure? UNI-LOC not only incorporated all Ten Essentials into our operations, we may have originated num-

bers two, three, and eight. And UNI-LOC was—and still is—
The Fail-Proof Enterprise.

Remember, all of the Essentials are directed at maximizing
owner–employee commitment and efficiency. If your company
utilizes all of these very basic, common sense Essentials—or as
many as possible—and your competitors don't, and your products and services are no better than theirs, you will bury them.
Your enterprise will be in business long after they are gone. And
that is what this exercise is all about.

The goals of the game are to build a successful, fail-proof
enterprise, to maintain it for as long as possible as an entrepreneurship to assure maximum growth and profitability, and then
to sell out to a wealthy bureaucracy and go fishing. When you
get bored, and you will get bored, do some market research,
discover a new product or service opportunity, and do it all over
again. That is what we entrepreneurs are destined to do. After
all, we're unemployable.

QUESTIONS & ANSWERS

QUESTIONS

Chapter 1

1. Besides being a risk taker, what is an entrepreneur?

2. How did the majority of large corporations begin?

3. In any enterprise, what does the presence of a middle-management level indicate?

4. Given the opportunity, can anyone become a true entrepreneur?

5. What is the essence of entrepreneurial performance?

6. If you were to start up a new company with all middle-management functions in place from the beginning, what is the most important thing you will need?

7. What are the main characteristics of large bureaucratic enterprises?

8. What is the most important single activity that plays the lead role in almost every business enterprise?

9. In a large bureaucratic business enterprise what is the one department that allows its members to operate almost as freely as an entrepreneur?

10. What are the main attributes of the entrepreneur?

Answers on page 251

Chapter 2

1. What should you expect from this book?

2. What is the main difference between entrepreneurs and the leaders of our nation's major corporations?

3. What is the single most important element for business success?

4. What type of people form the backbone of the capitalist system?

5. What was the near-fatal mistake I made with North American Aviation on the B-70 program? What was the lesson learned?

6. What principal side benefit did I receive as a result of being in sales?

7. What was the near-fatal mistake I made in my dealings with Convair, Pomona on the vacuum tube amplifier package? What was the lesson learned?

8. After reading this chapter, how do you feel about developing close relationships with your customers?

Answers on page 252

Chapter 3

1. What was the principal difference between my job at Oster and the one at NLS?

2. What was the main thrust of the NLS job?

3. If you want to progress in your career what must you often be prepared to do?

4. In the marketing part of my NLS job, what was my first task?

5. When is one of the most productive times of the day to make "cold" sales calls?

6. What is the primary function of market research?

7. What is the objective of gathering data from as many companies as possible when doing market research?

8. What was the main lesson learned in losing the seismic market to a new company?

Answers on page 254

Chapter 4

1. If you find yourself priced out of the marketplace for your current position, what are your best options?

2. What was the underlying problem with the application of water treatment chemicals?

3. What do you think the principal reasons were we decided to start UNI-LOC?

Answers on page 256

Chapter 5

1. What is one of the most important keys to the management of subordinates?

2. What do many management consultants do in the process of turning around a company's profitability?

3. What is lacking in most companies' sales forces?

4. What best describes NLS as a company?

5. To keep your company functioning as an entrepreneurial enterprise, what must you avoid?

6. What were the three obvious choices for financing UNI-LOC?

7. What proved to be the most important decision affecting UNI-LOC's future with respect to funding?

8. Why did I decide to commit UNI-LOC stock to my partners upfront, at the beginnings of the enterprise, instead of promising options in the future as they proved themselves?

Answers on page 257

Chapter 6

1. What was my nagging doubt about what we were attempting to do with our cooling water control system?

2. What was the truth about all pH analyzers that surfaced, thanks to my talk with Monsanto's Ed Thomason?

3. Without the combination of skills, training, and experiences we UNI-LOC partners had, do you think we could have solved our unexpected technical problems as satisfactorily and as quickly as we did?

Answers on page 259

Chapter 7

1. What could we have done differently before we were sued, with respect to the plaintiff's having been offered the same opportunity with the phone company that we had subsequently accepted?

2. Had we been financially structured like the typical start-up—that is, had we all put money into the pot and paid ourselves salaries —do you think we could have survived the financial burden of the lawsuit?

3. What action might we have taken earlier when we were sued?

4. Although unconventional, what was the reason the telephone company called our attention to the fact that we might increase our prices and establish an indemnification fund in case things went against us in the lawsuit?

Answers on page 259

Chapter 8

1. After our success with the telephone company, what was the biggest obstacle to our developing the "virgin" market for our cooling water control systems?

2. What was the second, and most important, innovation in the owner–management structure of UNI-LOC?

3. When UNI-LOC began to develop the cooling water control system market outside the telephone company, what best characterized the state of the commercial water treatment industry?

Answers on page 260

Chapter 9

1. What are the main considerations in establishing a company sales force versus a commissioned representative sales force?

2. How effective was UNI-LOC's "dealer" discount policy?

3. What are the guidelines for establishing sales rep commissions?

4. What are the schools of thought on patents pending versus patents being issued as quickly as possible?

5. What was the next logical step in sustaining UNI-LOC's growth?

Answers on page 261

Chapter 10

1. What was the purpose of limiting UNI-LOC's management structure to three levels?

2. What is the principal goal of Management By Objectives (MBO)?

3. What did behavioral expert Herzberg say about money?

4. What was the UNI-LOC innovation concerning employee wages?

5. What was yet another profit-sharing innovation UNI-LOC instituted?

6. How did I envision the differences between sales managers and marketing managers?

7. What was different about UNI-LOC's new offices?

Answers on page 263

Chapter 11

1. What was the main difference between the industrial pH analyzer market versus the commercial water treatment market?

2. What was the main obstacle delaying UNI-LOC's recognition by engineering-constructors as a legitimate supplier of pH analyzers for process industry new construction?

Answers on page 265

Chapter 12

1. Why did UNI-LOC's owners keep their salaries and bonuses at the lower end of electronic industry averages?

2. How did UNI-LOC's pH analyzers revolutionize some batch processes and other applications as well?

3. What were the major factors that lead us to decide to be acquired by Betz instead of proceeding with our plan to go public?

4. What was the innovation that made the Betz acquisition of UNI-LOC a reality?

5. Besides monetary, what is the other most important consideration in being acquired?

Answers on page 265

Chapter 13

1. What was the biggest single obstacle to establishing a European market for UNI-LOC's Model 1000 pH Analyzer?

Answer on page 267

Chapter 14

1. Who is best qualified to review and evaluate your "Intellectual Property Rights"?

2. Why was the defendant assessed treble damages in the UNI-LOC pH patent litigation?

3. What was the most important single characteristic of UNI-LOC's approach to sales?

4. Why did Betz sell UNI-LOC to Rosemont-Emerson?

5. How can aptitude tests, such as those administered by the Human Engineering Laboratory, help your business enterprise?

Answers on page 267

ANSWERS

Chapter 1

1. A state of being. A human condition. Once you cross the line to enterpreneurship, there is no going back. Entrepreneurial traits are often repressed, as they were with me. As long as that situation remains, you will have little contentment and, perhaps, emotional instability.

2. As entrepreneurial enterprises. The problem, however, is that those in charge today are not the same people who started the enterprise. Being bureaucrats, they feel threatened when confronted with entrepreneurial characteristics in their own employees. If they were clever, big company managers would keep those employees challenged to the point that they would never even dream of going off on their own and becoming competitors.

3. Bureaucracy. In the well-defined entrepreneurship there is little need for middle management until the enterprise has grown substantially. If there is only one owner, the day of bureaucratic reckoning will come much earlier. The more active the owner–partners the better chance of staving off the inevitable bureaucracy.

4. No. Anyone can try to be an entrepreneur, but if the inherent characteristics don't exist, he or she will be dissatisfied.

5. An entrepreneur is driven to perform as many tasks as necessary to get the job done, even if the aptitudes and skills aren't always ideal. An entrepreneur is willing to work as many hours per day as required for as long as it takes.

6. Lots of money. Personally, I prefer running lean in the beginning even if unlimited finances are available, as we did with TBI. It is silly and counterproductive to load a new enterprise down with more people than you need just to have a textbook bureaucratic organization in place.

7. Slow and often unresponsive, but safe. Aside from the integrity of the products or services, the slow response time of a bureaucracy, as compared to the entrepreneurship, is generally what makes it possible for the entrepreneurship to invade the bureaucracy's marketplace.

8. Sales. Sales in one form or another is the prime mover of any product or service business. And this includes merchandising, although to a lesser extent. Every enterprise must have income, and no matter how good the products or services, they can only sell themselves for so long.

9. Again, sales. The nature of selling, whether on salary or commission, is such that the results are visible for all to see. There is nowhere to hide. Because of that high risk exposure, salespeople are given more latitude to make their own decisions without running to the boss, provided they remain within the bounds of company policies. Sales is truly an entrepreneurial experience.

10. Drive and desire. Work ethic. High energy level. Vision. Impatience with mundane details. Distaste for routine, unnecessary meetings. Zero tolerance for misinformation. Eager and ready to do whatever needs to be done.

Chapter 2

1. How to structure and manage a new enterprise in such a way that failure isn't a probability or even a possibility unless you have substandard products or services, terrible management, or the worst possible luck. Although good luck is always helpful, this book minimizes that factor.

2. More often than not, entrepreneurs take the risks of getting into business with very little funding. Leaders of big companies, highly competent managers from a textbook standpoint who usually have

impeccable educational and experience credentials, have never had to manage an institution without adequate budgets and readily available funding at their disposal.

3. The quality of the products or services your company offers for sale. If your company is well-structured and offers good products or services, it can survive even with mediocre managers. Of course, to be fail-proof, it must have excellent management, sound structure, aggressive sales, and at least as good a product or service as the competition.

4. The entrepreneurs. Collectively, all of the entrepreneurial businesses in our nation probably have a combined gross dollar product larger than that of the largest corporations. Not only that, these entrepreneurial enterprises are likely to become the future corporate giants. It is easier for entrepreneurs to encroach on the markets dominated by large corporations than it is for large corporations to expand against each other.

5. I ignored the purchasing department. I just assumed everything was okay. For good reason, I always avoided exposing myself to purchasing too early because that was where my competitors tended to hang out. I always tried to be the quiet one, but in this case it almost backfired. I never made that mistake again.

6. Firsthand observation of the inner workings of the companies I worked for and of my customers' companies as well. Over time, I developed my organizational ideas as a result of my inner-sanctum exposures through my sales work. I was privy to many things that were otherwise private.

7. Relying too much on one group—engineering. Of course, I was well-acquainted with purchasing personnel and with the purchasing- engineering liaison—my golfing buddy—so it wasn't that I ignored them, as I had at North American. But I was so close to key engineers that I was afraid of offending them were my com-

pany the only one to bid a vacuum tube device. That was stupid! A specification is a specification, and it should be bid as written. Live and learn. Also, note how a careless remark, the one about the "car-in-the-driveway," dearly cost my competitor.

8. Despite what happened to me at Convair, Pomona, I still believe in establishing and maintaining close personal relationships with my customers. I represented my customer's interests in dealing with Oster as I represented Oster's interests in dealing with my customer. Benefits have to be mutual if profitable relationships are to be maintained.

Chapter 3

1. While both jobs involved sales, my work at NLS was mostly marketing, which is why I took it in the first place. At Oster, I often was involved in exciting new developments, but our market was always the same—the government. At NLS, I searched out new markets for yet undeveloped capabilities, which resulted in new products. This was genuine firsthand market research. Experience that served me well.

2. New markets for existing products if possible, but at no time did I myself ever sell an off-the-shelf NLS product in a new market. New markets in the Gulf Coast called for new products, but we didn't know what those would be. It was my job to find out.

3. Move. Follow the opportunities. Be as mobile as possible if you are on a career path that is the least bit volatile, such as sales. Turning down an opportunity merely because you may not want to leave a comfortable area or because you are too tied down will almost certainly dead-end your career.

4. To pick the brains of the R&D directors in the oil, gas, chemical, and petrochemical industries. To try to find some common problems among them. I found many possibilities besides those we

exploited at NLS, but they didn't fit NLS's capabilities. There is always an oasis of opportunity out there for somebody, but you have to find those that fit your capabilities. Most companies wouldn't have funded an effort like mine in the Gulf Coast, and they would have missed the boat. Researching markets with computer jockeys playing "what if" games only gets you less than half the story: You need an intelligent, aggressive, sales-experienced person out in the field. That is where the markets are.

5. After the work day is over or almost over. The key people you want to reach often can't see outsiders during the day because they are too busy. I generated some excellent sales relationships this way—while my competitors were off partaking of "happy hour."

6. Shut up and listen. Take copious notes and spend lots of time looking for significant trends. If several potential customers have the same or a similar problem, a market exists.

7. Again, trends that hopefully can fit your company's capabilities. But remember, your company will often have to extend itself in order to take advantage of that "trend." It is not like finding a bird's nest on the ground. If it were easy, someone else would have done it already.

8. Don't downplay the findings and opinions of your own marketing or salespeople. They are on the front lines. If you are going to invest in market research and the person you are investing in has a proven track record in sales, as I had, listen to that person! And don't habitually respond negatively to new ideas. The small computer I wanted NLS to develop had enormous application potentials other than seismic, and I already had the seismic market locked up just waiting for such a device. That little computer was SDS's only product, and Xerox paid more than $90 million for the company, several times what NLS was worth.

Chapter 4

1. To go into business for yourself as I finally did; to work through a good personnel firm—a headhunter, which is a good way to go; to continue to search the job market yourself as I unsuccessfully did for awhile; or to fib about your last salary level. I don't recommend the latter unless you are sure you will stay with your new employer at a reduced salary and work your way up. Of course, if you are caught, you will have a lot of explaining to do, but by then your new employer may be willing to overlook your deception. I wouldn't do that myself, but it is an option.

    I gave up too soon. I could have used the Buchanan method again and written letters to the presidents of twenty-five good companies and had a bunch of interviews. It always works if you do it right. Corporate presidents will read a well-written one-page job solicitation and will forward it to the appropriate person. Do not include a resume in your letters to the presidents. Your interviewer will ask for that. Your inquiry to the presidents should simply state: (1) the job—don't use the word "position"—you are seeking; (2) something positive about your abilities and attitudes; and, (3) why you want to work for that company. Period!

2. No control. Chemicals were manually added to cooling water if and when the maintenance staff thought about it, and if it didn't interfere with unscheduled emergencies. The same was true with bleed-off. It was an accident waiting to happen, and it always did, usually at the least opportune time.

3. Bell Telephone as our first customer, the unqualified support of our families, and timing. In retrospect, I see we would have been remiss not to have taken the chance when a blue-chip customer offered to support us in one way or another. Even though we appreciated that, we were aware we would be exposed to a different technology, largely unknown to us. That was scary, and it made the decision to dive in and lay it all on the line difficult.

Chapter 5

1. Successful management is by the consent of your subordinates, through leadership. Employees, or even partners for that matter, will not do their best work unless they have consciously or sub-consciously consented to be managed. This holds true no matter if you are the sole owner or merely a straw boss. Management by directive will ultimately fail.

2. Cut the workforce and reduce overhead to quickly enhance profits. This works in the short term but it can be frightfully expensive in the long run if trained employees are allowed to get away. Consultants offer little help in developing new markets or products, which is necessary to avoid stagnancy, especially during a recession. What amazes me is how long it takes big companies to adjust to business cycle downturns since we have always had them and always will. Their losses can be staggering before meaningful action is taken, usually in the form of cuts. This reinforces my thesis that MBAs and accountants are not able to give management anything useful other than data produced by outside sources. The marketing methods of big companies are fundamentally flawed.

3. Professional credentials, or people with higher education. Unfortunately, those who have "born" sales and management aptitudes also have personality aptitudes that make it difficult to study for extended periods in isolation. It is paradoxical that the "born" ideal personality trait for sales, teaching, and management is one and the same. Slogging through a typical college curriculum for four years is difficult, in terms of patience, for those with that particular "personality" aptitude. Many "born" managers, sales-people, and teachers quit school before they get their credentials, which stigmatizes them as second-class citizens.

4. An entrepreneurship with progressive management attitudes and objectives. Until UNI-LOC, NLS was possibly the first high-tech

company that purposely identified itself as an entrepreneurial enterprise, and it knew how to remain one.

5. Middle management! Its formation is the first sign that entrepreneurs are losing their grip on some key aspects of running the organization. Remember, middle managers are rarely content: They have no place to go advancement-wise until the enterprise becomes a bona fide bureaucracy. Middle management is the principal breeding ground for company politics and discontent.

6. (1) To finance it myself, paying salaries, and offering future stock options based upon the performances of my partners. (2) Venture capital. (3) All partner–participants contributing money into a pool and then drawing salaries. Still another possibility might have been to sell stock upfront to silent investors, but this would have meant exploiting our friends and relatives, and we weren't sure enough of our future to consider doing that.

7. Loaning the company money myself, interest-free, for expenses, supplies, and overhead, and then requiring all participants to work eighteen months without any salary in exchange for a stock ownership pledge. I knew we would either prove ourselves or quit within that timeframe. I was thinking only of short-term survival until we were absolutely sure one way or the other, and I wanted to keep our financial picture in the forefront at all times. This guaranteed that everyone would work long hours seven days a week without my having to say anything.

8. Promises of "future" stock distribution more often than not fall flat, and anybody who leaves a good job on a pie-in-the-sky stock option promise is crazy. The problem with new start-up companies that need the services of a core group of "volunteers," or lower-paid subordinates, is that volunteer-subordinates are never content until their ownership promises are confirmed. I have seen many companies with low morale and high turnover for just that reason—and all of them failed. I wanted no part of that.

Chapter 6

1. Why hadn't a reliable cooling water control system been built before? From my experiences in aerospace and with the Gulf Coast industries, I had a good idea of what was available in industrial control technology. Therefore, something was really afoul with what we were attempting to do. But what?

2. That pH analyzers had always been a pain, but one that could be lived with if the users could afford the technicians to recalibrate them several times a day. The Gulf Coast process industries just accepted that. For them, it was an improvement over the old days, when they had to grab samples every hour and run them to the laboratory for pH tests. Had we known this, we probably would not have accepted Pacific Telephone's offer to develop a cooling water control system for them because pH was by far our most threatening problem. What is the lesson here? Sometimes you are better off not knowing the reasons why you might fail.

3. Absolutely not. This proves that a well-balanced partnership is better than a sole proprietorship. Had I been the only owner, I could never have hired anyone who had the required dedication that Phil Cardeiro had, not to mention Ted Barben and Jack Horner.

Chapter 7

1. Perhaps taken a license from the plaintiff to use his corrosion rate measurement device, even though we couldn't use it. We still had to design and build our own. Had we already had our corrosion interlock patent in hand we probably could have worked out a cross license at that time, but our interlock patent didn't issue until three years later.

2. No. Had we been paying ourselves salaries, we would not have been able to survive the expenses of the lawsuit without an outside capital infusion—and that is impossible to get in the face of a

pending lawsuit. As it was, we had money in the bank when we were hit with the lawsuit and after it was settled, and I still had almost all of my own capital intact in case we might need it. By the way, the total amount I loaned the company never exceeded $12,000.

3. I might have contacted the plaintiff's president sooner and attempted to work out some kind of compromise. But it is doubtful that the end result would have been as good for UNI-LOC as it turned out to be. The plaintiff had to be convinced we were in the fight to stay and that the phone company was standing with us.

4. Although the phone company liked us and we had the highest regard for it as a customer, it wasn't altruistic. We were the key to what it needed in order to save a lot of money and to avoid lost time. In the phone company's mind it was cost effective for us to increase our prices by 10 percent for indemnification, which was legally in line with its internal policy. Being a quasi-utility, it was imperative that its interests be protected in a way that was consistent with company policy. But in spite of the fact that the phone company wanted and needed our systems, I was awed by the ease and confidence with which they handled the lawsuit crises and their business dealings with us. I can't help wondering if things are as good today since the break-up of that truly marvelous, technologically innovative leader of all leaders, Ma Bell.

Chapter 8

1. There was no established or ready market for water treatment control equipment. The market was jealously controlled by water treatment chemical suppliers who knew that automation would reduce chemical usage and, subsequently, customer dependence upon them.

2. My relinquishing majority stock ownership in UNI-LOC to my partners. I cannot overstate the importance of that move. I credit

it for the fact we had no serious difficulties among us—ever. All of our energies were spent on achieving company objectives. No jealousies. No politics. No doubts. Maximum efficiency.

3. The "commercial" chemical suppliers were in chaos and disarray. It was dog-eat-dog, with nobody getting decent results. Of course, the main fault wasn't with the chemical suppliers. Their chemicals couldn't do the job unless they got into the cooling water, and their customer-users did a horrible job in that regard. But the chemical suppliers did not make any serious efforts to improve the status quo by pioneering control systems themselves.

Chapter 9

1. Basically, there are three options and two call for in-house sales forces. The first option is perhaps the most traditional: an in-house company sales force. The salespeople make in-person customer calls in assigned territories. This is the best kind of sales force if your products are complicated and require liaison between the customer and your home office.

    Another traditional method is to use commissioned sales representatives in various regions throughout the country. The advantages here are that you don't pay them until your products are sold. No salaries. No expenses. If your products are reasonably straightforward and require few "special" modifications, rep sales will work very well. However, unless you visit your sales rep network often, you will only receive a limited percentage of their selling time.

    The newest, and lowest cost, sales method is also an in-house, company-owned sales force. This one does no traveling, but lots of telephone work. First, you advertise heavily, broadcasting your Website address. Then, exhibit as many product specifications as you can on your Website—and prominently display your toll-free telephone number for additional information, prices, and delivery information. This is where the actual sales are made—over the phone. Remember, somewhere along the line you must have salespeople selling your products. Advertising and the Internet alone will rarely do it unless the customers have already made up their minds to purchase your product prior to visiting the Web.

2. Very effective. That was our best entrée into the water treatment chemical world besides the custom instruments we manufactured for Betz. Since our "dealers" were both commercial and industrial chemical suppliers, it was the perfect marriage between equipment people—our reps—and the chemical salespeople. We had finally bridged the gap.

3. Make them as high as you possibly can, at the top end of industry commission levels. Like lawyers, reps' time is their stock and trade. It is only natural they will spend the most time selling the products that carry the best commissions with the best sales potential in the long run. Reps will invest time laying groundwork—such as calling on consulting engineers—but before they do, they must have a good commission rate with an easier sell down the road.

4. The popular school believes that patent protection is better after the patent has issued. They think that the mere fact there is a patent number on a device is enough to scare off most infringers. The minority school, and the one I support, believes that protection can often be better while patents are pending. With pending patents, your potential infringers have no idea how strong the coverage will be until they can see which of your claims the patent office has allowed. If an infringer invests heavily in copying your product while it is in the pending stage, and then you get a strong patent, the infringer knows he will have to cease and desist or face serious monetary consequences. Once your patent has issued, it is in the public domain, and everyone can see which claims have been approved. If you have a weak patent, your potential

competitors will likely be able to circumvent your claims and essentially copy your product.

5. To break out the pH analyzer portion of our cooling water control systems, redesign it for heavy-duty industrial applications, and market it as a separate instrument. The potential market in retrofitting the thousands of 25-year-old pH analyzers in current use was staggering, not to mention the market for new applications that could utilize "on-stream" pH control.

Chapter 10

1. To keep the chain of command as short as possible, which ensures that communication is excellent. And to postpone the creation of middle management, which would establish a fourth company level. Each added level buries an organization that much deeper in bureaucratic red tape. Remember, entrepreneurial enterprises are extremely efficient as compared to bureaucratic enterprises— and efficiency is an important survival tool when competing against bigger organizations.

2. To give middle managers the idea that if they identify additional opportunities within their job classifications, and develop those opportunities to the fullest extent, the path to upper management will be more clear. It isn't a bad idea, but it is bureaucratic. The clever ones will try to expand their jobs into gray areas to become more prominent. This, however, breeds politics and muddles the issue of individual objectives versus company objectives. Those objectives should not conflict.

3. Money is a dissatisfier. No one is ever satisfied with one's salary or bank account. The quest for money becomes a gratification substitute for those who do not enjoy their work, or feel underappreciated. This is understandable. And management should

constantly work to find ways, other than monetary, to show individual performance appreciation. Again, it is important to identify your employees' strongest skills and to place them in jobs where they will be more productive—and most happy.

4.   Not using time clocks, and not paying by the hour. We set up a salary structure that everyone could see. We had no set "performance review" periods. Our employees got raises when their lead persons felt they had earned a raise. We had a good medical plan, but we would continue to carry ill employees on salary for as long as we could after verifying the illness. With no time clock, what did we do about employee tardiness? We made it clear we would not tolerate it.

5.   A week off with pay between Christmas and New Year's Day plus a bonus package. The bonuses were not based on salary level. We wanted most of the bonus money to go to the troops. When you think about it, the week's pay plus bonus probably paid for our employees' Christmas; having the week off gave them plenty of time to shop, visit loved ones, and enjoy the holidays. This was an employee-relations coup. The best form of profit-sharing.

6.   Sales managers are typically involved with the short range—today's products and services. What they sell today pays for tomorrow's R&D and all other expenditures. Marketing managers are involved with the long range—tomorrow's markets and the new products for those markets. I believe that marketing people should be groomed from salespeople, not MBAs or the like, even though marketing is considered a research function. Marketers must have a hands-on feel for sales. This is what keeps them focused on marketing objectives. Out of this exercise we want to discover something new to sell and someplace new to sell it.

7.   The bullpen without cubicles or partitions. I know this sounds like a minor item but until you've tried it, even in a big office, you can never appreciate its advantages.

Chapter 11

1. The commercial water treatment market for UNI-LOC control systems didn't exist as an established market. We had to create it. The pH analyzer market was everywhere, but it was dominated by two, sometimes three, old-line companies that manufactured many other products. They were giants compared to UNI-LOC, and they had years of influence because they were good. UNI-LOC came along with a superior product, but the inertia that had to be overcome was formidable—and understandable.

2. We hadn't been around long enough. Engineering-constructors continued to specify the older pH analyzers, which they had successfully specified for 25 years, because it was safe. They had a legal obligation to their clients that took precedence over any temptation they might have as engineers to use leading-edge, state-of-the-art instrumentation.

Chapter 12

1. Because we wanted to maximize our profits in anticipation of the day we would either go public or sell out to or merge with another company. We established that goal in the beginning.

    You can't have it both ways in business: that is, you can't pay yourselves big salaries and bonuses, which reduce company profits, and expect a bonanza when sell-out or public-issue time comes. And remember, salaries and bonuses are taxed at ordinary income tax rates while profits from the sale of the company or your stock are taxed at capital gain rates. Corporation tax rates can also be high so you must hire a professional for tax planning. This is when a great comptroller is worth his or her weight in gold.

2. In some liquid and slurry processes UNI-LOC pH analyzers eliminated the old batch method. This required a reliable, accurate, stable, and rugged pH analyzer. Many new pH applications were

actually old applications that were so nasty, so full of contaminates, that older pH instrumentation wouldn't work. Samples had to be taken at regular intervals and the company lab would run pH tests; manual adjustments of the chemicals would be made. Many of these pH applications finally became possible "on-stream" thanks to UNI-LOC control.

3.   Betz had just gone public, which meant its stock selling price was still low in relation to its true value compared to most companies on the exchange. Betz was loaded with cash before going public, so it wasn't likely to be hurting for money any time soon, even though they had spent a bundle on new headquarters, labs, and factory. An eighty-year track record coupled with a modern, aggressive approach to doing business is a rare combination. In retrospect, we may have made more money over a much longer period by going public because UNI-LOC was a real cherry. We were consistently highly profitable and could have remained so for years even without major new technical achievements. But our lives wouldn't have been the same. We would have become a bureaucracy.

4.   The earn-out. Without the chance to at least double our selling price over that three-year period, we would not have sold under any circumstances. As it turned out, with the Betz stock each of us held to the end of the earn-out period plus the final two-year SEC restriction, the total value was ten times more than the value of our original deal. The stock split twice before the end of the earn-out, we received the earn-out stock (which equaled the number of shares of our original transaction), and then the whole thing split again. Over time the stock returned to the split price. All that took place over a six-year period.

5.   Compatibility. This is why selling or merging your company should be done cautiously and slowly. You must spend sufficient time with your suitors to test the consistency between what they say and what they do. In the beginning, all parties are on their

best behavior; they express themselves carefully in both meetings and casual conversation. But it's over a few drinks after hours or on the golf course or the tennis court that you learn the true character of the people you are thinking of working with or for.

Chapter 13

1. The German PTB tests and the British ICI tests. But these only affected instrumentation used in hazardous environments such as gas, chemical, and petrochemical applications—our largest potential market. But we still made sales in the papermaking industry and the distillery and yeast-making industries. The PTB and ICI so-called safety tests perplexed us because the safety record in the U.S. was every bit as good as in Europe, and our instruments were all UL-approved and had passed additional tests for extra-hazardous applications. The conclusion I came to was that those tests were simply punitive, roadblocks designed to give Europe's manufacturers time to catch-up with foreign innovation. And being socialist, European governments love to employ lots of bureaucrats with little else to do than stick their noses into everything.

Chapter 14

1. A reputable patent attorney who also knows copyright law. Trade secrets are another matter: The only way to protect those is to keep them secret.

2. Because it continued to sell its allegedly infringing pH analyzers after having been sued, before the suit went to patent court. During that four-year interim, the defendant sold a lot of pH instruments. Interestingly, UNI-LOC's weakest patent claim was the one that sunk the defendant. Ironic. Damages were in the millions.

3. Thorough market evaluation and planning. Tenacity. We never
    gave up. We refused to take no for an answer until the order was
    already in our competitor's hands.

4. When Phil Cardeiro left UNI-LOC some years after I did, Betz made
    the mistake of replacing him with one of its own mid-level in-house
    guys who happened to be at loose ends. Barben was passed over,
    but he never wanted to be president anyway. Wes Coombe was
    the logical choice and could have worn the president's hat while
    performing his other duties, as I had. Even Carl Frova, who wasn't
    quite ready for a president's job, would have been a far better
    choice. The new man added nothing to management's depth and
    was a politicking caretaker. When Barben left to join me in Neva-
    da, Betz was strapped for proven, top-notch instrument company
    managers. I think that discouraged them and laid the groundwork
    for their selling UNI-LOC to a high-tech equipment company.

    The only failing on Cardeiro's part was that he had not groomed
    a first-class engineering replacement for himself when he was pro-
    moted to president. Nobody replaced me in marketing either. It
    was a ship without a rudder, and by then a bureaucracy.

5. By testing the partners and employees of a new enterprise, the
    Human Engineering Lab can show all involved the capacities in
    which they can best serve the company—and be a helluva lot hap-
    pier doing it. This is especially important if people are going to
    wear more than one hat, as we did at UNI-LOC. If you know where
    possible aptitude conflicts might arise, you can take steps to avoid
    those conflicts. The object is to dovetail as many strong aptitudes
    as possible so that all the bases are covered by the best candidates.
    You also need to know who has "management" aptitude and, as
    we discussed, the vocabulary levels of the partners. Vocabulary is
    one aptitude that is "learned"—not innate—and one everyone can
    and should improve. Vocabulary is knowledge, and a high level is
    required for business success.

 **Bob Thomas** was raised and educated in Southern California. Following military service in World War II, where he was a U.S. Army Air Corps aviation cadet, he returned to school, graduating from UCLA. After working for six years as an aircraft engineer in the fledgling aerospace industry, he entered the field of high-tech sales, selling specialized technical products to the aerospace industry, eventually becoming a sales and marketing manager.

Seven years later, he co-founded UNI-LOC, the high-tech company about which this book is written, and became its first president and CEO. UNI-LOC is now a division of Emerson Process (formerly Emerson Electric), a Fortune 500 company. A few years after selling UNI-LOC, he co-founded TBI, another high-tech company similar to UNI-LOC. He was TBI's first president and CEO as well. TBI was eventually sold to Bailey Controls–McDermott company, another Fortune 500 company; it is now part of the Swiss conglomerate ABB.

After moving to Carson City, Nevada, his adopted hometown, Thomas founded Comstock Aviation. He was appointed to the state welfare board and to the employee management relations board and served four years. He was elected to the Carson City School Board, serving four years, and then to the Nevada State Legislature, serving three terms. He also founded the Carson City Airport Authority and is currently serving his second term as chairman. He is in his nineteenth year of public service.

From 1996 through 2001 Thomas was a featured weekly columnist on the op-ed page of the *Nevada Appeal*, Nevada's oldest newspaper. He still writes his column as time permits.

Peer Reviews of *The Fail-Proof Enterprise*

Bob Thomas turns the wisdom drawn from his entrepreneurial life into an owner/investor aid for the sales-driven enterprise. His approach is "fabulous."

In the literal sense, Bob Thomas spins a fable that carries the genetic code for this entrepreneurial success mode.

In the moral sense, Bob Thomas uses humor to make the fundamental "unemployability" of the rugged individualist into the bedrock of wealth creation.

In the development sense, Mr. Thomas takes his perfect reader through all stages of Erickson's maturation hierarchy—and then reminds them that the potential for doing it all again is always there.

In the spiritual sense, the sense of "doing good work," Bob Thomas re-establishes the character of the business leader as the key to his final contribution to the free market economy and thus also to the ecology of independence.

All in all, Bob Thomas affirms the American Way in his own way. He declares his devotion to western (not Yankee) pragmatism, illustrating for those who would follow in his footpath how to find their own Northwest Passage. A breeze to read, full of counsel to heed.

—*Dr. Jefferson A. Stewart*
Chairman, Advisory Council of the
American Society for Competitiveness (ASC)

I spent forty-two years with a Fortune 500 company—the last twelve as CEO—and I think Bob Thomas has it right.

His book, *The Fail-Proof Enterprise*, is a must-read for every young man and woman in today's business schools. In truth, every college student would benefit from reading of his life experiences. Even some of us old timers might learn something.

Bob Thomas knows what it takes to be a successful entrepreneur.

—*W. E. LaMothe*
Chairman Emeritus & past CEO, Kellogg Company